'Rarely does a book contain such breadth and depth of information, that is based on current research and proven techniques. Reading Margareth's book is comparable to completing an advanced degree in the field and practice of leadership. Each page contains information that is worth digesting and soaking in. As a person, Margareth is a force of nature; her book follows suit: it is strong, lively, unchallengeable, and full of energy.'

– Kathleen Stinnet, MCC, executive coach, and co-author of The Extraordinary Coach

'Currently, at a time when leadership is in greater demand than ever before, it is especially refreshing to read Margareth's fresh and insightful ideas. Leadership is not a trick or a show, nor is it performance. Real leadership is based on content and authenticity; that is to say, it is based on competence, passion, and organizational needs. The CPO model provides a fantastic benchmark by which every leader can consider how to further increase their own impact, as well as how their leadership can have a contagious effect on others."

– Roger Dassen, CFO ASML

'This book is published at a time where the world is experiencing a pandemic, and it is also evident that a special kind of leadership is required to navigate during a crisis period, be this crisis a health or economic situation This means that we cannot proceed with 'business as usual'. Leaders' behaviours should reflect the new mind set, one that is focused on driving a vision that inspires confidence in others and leads the way.'

– Professor Zwelinzima Ndevu, Stellenbosch University, South Africa

'A true invitation to step out of our comfort zone and be the change to "Make Shift Happen"!'

– Maarten de Vries, CFO Akzo Nobel

'I have known Margareth for almost a decade and her intellect, enthusiasm, and powerful communication have always impressed me in our many discussions—both internally and externally with clients in India—on augmenting clients' leadership pipeline using Zenger Folkman's leadership interventions. Her approach, which is based on the award-winning development tools from Zenger Folkman on enhancing personal leadership development, has helped many top organizations in India, both multinational and domestic. This book is a great guide, one that is buttressed with examples that enable leaders to understand their sweet spot and which facilitate their personal transition and their organisation's transition through compassionate and inclusive leadership using scientific leadership tools.'

– Rontu Basu, Co-Founder/Partner Quest Partners, India

T0317130

Making Shift Happen

Directing Impact

Margareth de Wit

Amsterdam University Press

This is an Academica LifeLong Learning and Amsterdam University Press publication. Academica is a knowledge institution that offers flexible and high-quality education. At Academica, leaders and professionals are supported in increasing their personal effectiveness and in developing a long-term vision that ensures strong employee engagement, an open and action-oriented culture, and continuous improvement of results supported by targeted innovation. Academica is the strategic certified partner of Zenger and Folkman's global leadership programme in the Netherlands.

The timeline and chapter openings were drawn by Oliver Caviglioli.

Photo author cover: Gowan Genìs, Studio GO1

Cover design: Academia bv
Layout design: Crius Group, Hulshout

ISBN	978 94 6372 026 7
e-ISBN	978 90 4855 419 5
NUR	800
DOI	10.5117/9789463720267

For my father

My father has had a considerable influence on how I see the world and my own life, but especially on how I act and make choices. I dedicate this book to him. He was my great example of how to live as a human being in this complex world. Until his death he was able to fascinate me daily with his boundless energy and unconditional love. 'Don't get annoyed, just marvel,' was his adage. I try to convey his message with the same positive energy.

Table of Contents

Timeline

Confucius | 551 BCE–479 BCE

Success always depends on careful preparation; without that preparation, failure is a fact.

Niccolò Machiavelli | 1469-1527

The best leaders are loved and feared, but because it is difficult to unite both in one person, the next best option is to be feared as a leader.

Thomas Carlyle | 1795-1881

The history of the world is but the biography of great men.

Frederick Taylor | 1856-1915

In the past the man has been first; in the future the system must be first.

Max Weber | 1864-1920

Charismatic leadership is authority based on the leader's personal qualities and the recognition thereof by their followers.

Bertrand Russell | 1872-1970

The whole problem with the world is that fools and fanatics are always so certain of themselves, and wiser people so full of doubt.

Simone de Beauvoir | 1908-1986

One is not born, but rather becomes, a woman.

Abraham Maslow | 1908-1970

If you only have a hammer, you tend to see every problem as a nail.

Peter Drucker | 1909-2005

Culture eats strategy for breakfast.

John W. Gardner | 1912-2002

Pity the leader caught between unloving critics and uncritical lovers.

Nelson Mandela | 1918-2013

May your choices reflect your hopes, not your fears.

Thomas Kuhn | 1922-1996

We see the world in terms of our theories.

Jim Rohn | 1930-2009

The enemy of great is good.

Jack Zenger | 1931

Greatness is not caused by the absence of weakness.

Umberto Eco | 1932-2016

I belong to a lost generation and am comfortable only in the company of others who are lost and lonely.

Jack Welch | 1935-2020

If you want to change the culture of an organization, change the way it develops its leaders.

Richard Petty | 1937

Confidence is the factor that turns thoughts into judgments about what we are capable of, and that then transforms those judgments into action.

Jesse Jackson | 1941

Inclusion is not a matter of political correctness. It is the key to growth.

Stephen Kern | 1943

Humanity has never strived to slow down.

Daniel Goleman | 1946

People need to be smarter with their emotions.

Anders Ericsson | 1947-2020

Deliberate Practice makes perfect.

John C. Maxwell | 1947

Leadership is not about titles, positions, or flowcharts. It is about one life influencing another.

Peter Senge | 1947

A learning organization is an organization that is continually expanding its capacity to create its future.

Jaap van Muijen | 1960

Leadership is shaped in the process between the personality of the leader, the characteristics of the followers, and those of the situation.

Otto Scharmer | 1961

The business that leaders are in today, is the business of transforming awareness... There is deep longing for more meaning, for connections.

Paul J. Zak | 1962

Trust is kind of this economic lubricant. When trust is high, morale is high... Higher trust environments produce individuals who are happier.

Frederic Laloux | 1969

In the new organizations, management is becoming a way to really bring out the best in people, where trust is given and where humanity is the focus. This ensures work environments that are inspired, goal-oriented and productive.

Foreword

This is a unique book. A quick glance at it may lead you to believe that it is merely one more book on the subject of leadership and leadership development. But that is not exactly what it is. The author's thesis is that the future depends on our ability to make appropriate transitions occur efficiently and effectively. Her aim is to prepare the reader to be a force in making these important shifts happen.

But it isn't the thesis of the book that alone distinguishes this work. We think it is the ability of the author to bring an unusually broad perspective to the topic. We are honored that she has referenced our research and writings. One of the facts that our research highlights is the notion of powerful combinations. The idea is simple. One force or element by itself often has modest influence, but when put together with another element, these become an extremely potent force. For example, gunpowder and a spark make a powerful combination.

This book showers the reader with several powerful combinations. For example, it is at once a very personal book, with references to her family, her business, and her academic experiences. That is combined with research and quotations from a wide variety of scholars in multiple disciplines.

The book is a practical field guide, full of concrete examples of activities that enable the practitioner to help organizations and individuals make transitions. Yet, at the same time, it contains bundles of excellent theory and models that help explain the process of change. This is another powerful combination.

This work is also a fascinating combination of the timely and timeless. It cites examples of the impact of the world pandemic in year 2020. However, alongside these references to current events are insightful discourses on ancient philosophers. This combination of modern science juxtaposed with the best thinking from the past is another powerful combination.

Change and transitions can be viewed from widely different perspectives. It can be approached from an individual, psychological perspective. It can also be viewed from a much broader sociological and organizational viewpoint. This author almost simultaneously does both. The outcome is a far more insightful and useful treatise, if compared to one that primarily used only one of these perspectives.

We could go on, but we hope that the point is made. This is an eclectic book, written in a way that incorporates many dimensions. That's what makes it unique. We promise the reader, you are about to embark on a good 'read'.

Jack Zenger and Joe Folkman
Authors of more than seven bestselling leadership and leadership development books, and founders of the award-winning Zenger Folkman consultancy.

Confucius | 551 BCE–479 BCE

Success always depends on careful preparation; without that preparation, failure is a fact.

Niccolò Machiavelli | 1469-1527

Thomas Carlyle | 1795-1881

Frederick Taylor | 1856-1915

Max Weber | 1864-1920

Bertrand Russell | 1872-1970

Simone de Beauvoir | 1908-1986

Abraham Maslow | 1908-1970

Peter Drucker | 1909-2005

John W. Gardner | 1912-2002

Nelson Mandela | 1918-2013

May your choices reflect your hopes, not your fears.

Thomas Kuhn | 1922-1996

Jim Rohn | 1930-2009

Jack Zenger | 1931

Umberto Eco | 1932-2016

Jack Welch | 1935-2020

Richard Petty | 1937

Jesse Jackson | **1941**

Stephen Kern | 1943

Daniel Goleman | 1946

Anders Ericsson | 1947-2020

John C. Maxwell | 1947

Peter Senge | 1947

Jaap van Muijen | 1960

Preface

Success always depends on careful preparation;
without that preparation, failure is a fact.
– Confucius (551 BC–479 BC)

Life is a journey of discovery for everyone. Sometimes it presents us with unexpected, beautiful moments, sometimes it confronts us with experiences of deep pain and disbelief. Often, we already have some life experience by the time we realize how certain mechanisms work, what the impact of our actions are, and how other people can affect us. In the search for how we can best get together and collaborate with other people, we are increasingly aware of how 'contagious' the knowledge and energy we transfer to others can be. Just think of people like Nelson Mandela and Barack Obama – how infectious their behaviours have been and how powerful their influence remains today. Or think of certain other events and experiences that are remembered with such pain and disbelief due to the attitude of leaders such as Hitler and Stalin, or the impact of the slave traders on our current society.

In a time when everything is within reach and nothing can be hidden, and when imagery and sound can be manipulated or distorted so easily, there is an increasing need to take direct control of what we have in this world in both our professional and our private lives.

In the twenty-first century, we look with different eyes at everything we use and the way we organize it; for example, just think of our energy sources, the way we travel, and how we use our possessions. The means by which we can best use our resources is an important political and social issue. However, such utilization goes much further than, for example, the transition to using solar and wind energy as renewable energy resources. Should we, for example, continue with our current substantial consumption of energy? And, on a more personal level, what are the limits of the commitment and energy we put into our work? You can only spend your time once: and, in asking these questions, we see that we want to do more and more in less and less time. This creates pressure in regard to how we spend our time, and therefore places considerable strain on individuals. What was once a classic dilemma for people in their thirties – 'what should I do with my life?' – is now a theme that engages more and more people from an earlier age, and is often prominently featured on people's personal agendas. 'What am I responsible for?', 'What can I really take responsibility for?', 'What choices do I have?', and 'What do I want to, and what can I achieve?' This shows the transition from a careless 'things will go the way they will' mentality to a 'What can I do to contribute and help in this complex world?' mentality.

In organizations, too, we now arrive at a point at which making a transition is necessary. We understand that we can and should relate to one another in a different way. But, as with all transitions, we are sometimes anxious or hesitant when trying to realize this in practice. Transition also requires choices as to where we should be heading: i.e., the process of transformation itself. **Transition** is about rules, laws, and systems. However, making a **transformation** necessarily concerns people's attitudes and behaviours and is, therefore, complicated, and unruly.

> *May your choices reflect your hopes, not your fears.*
> – Nelson Mandela (1918–2013)

Despite still offering the ostensible safety of predictability, handbooks for established job profiles and HR protocols with rules dictated in great detail are increasingly losing their power – 'I know exactly what to do; if I do it according to the rules, I will be doing it right'. However, such prescribed standard organizational processes no longer suffice to allow people to work together in order to achieve desired results, and this concerns both people and organizations. The 'lean and mean' approach, which led us to clean up bureaucratic processes from the 1990s onwards, has reached its tipping point, and now we are in danger of our quality being reduced.

Statements by philosophers, sociologists, psychologists, economists, political leaders, CEOs, religious leaders – as well as anyone else able to 'take the stage' – influence our ideas and the way we see and experience things on a daily basis. Formal leaders harness the power of contagion using their knowledge, ideas, and energy. We should *all* be more aware of the daily effects we have, as well as how we could use these to a greater extent in the future. Organizations' search for better interactions by using everyone's knowledge and skills is the key to understanding how we can make our own impact successful. The time of 'them versus us' has passed; now we are all responsible for a new transition and making the *shift* happen.

On the basis of my professional experiences over the past 33 years, as well as in the context of available scientific research, I describe the mechanisms by which professionals – both formal as well as informal leaders[1] – can create an impact. Leadership is for everyone in the organization. I want to challenge you and provide you with tools you need to enable a conscious transition in your personal leadership, because it is worth making the difference for everyone.

Confucius | 551 BCE–479 BCE

Niccolò Machiavelli | 1469-1527

The best leaders are loved and feared, but because it is difficult to unite both in one person, the next best option is to be feared as a leader.

Thomas Carlyle | 1795-1881

Frederick Taylor | 1856-1915

Max Weber | 1864-1920

Bertrand Russell | 1872-1970

Simone de Beauvoir | 1908-1986

Abraham Maslow | 1908-1970

Peter Drucker | 1909-2005

John W. Gardner | 1912-2002

Nelson Mandela | **1918-2013**

Thomas Kuhn | 1922-1996

Jim Rohn | 1930-2009

Jack Zenger | 1931

Umberto Eco | 1932-2016

Jack Welch | 1935-2020

Richard Petty | 1937

Jesse Jackson | **1941**

Stephen Kern | 1943

Daniel Goleman | 1946

Anders Ericsson | 1947-2020

John C. Maxwell | 1947

Peter Senge | 1947

Jaap van Muijen | 1960

Otto Scharmer | 1961

Paul J. Zak | 1962

Frederic Laloux | 1969

Introduction: The playing field

When you smile, the world smiles with you.
– James H. Fowler (1970, American social scientist) and Nicholas A. Christakis
(1962, Greek-American sociologist and physician)

If you are able to count yourself a happy person, then you can thank your partner and your friends. While you are thanking them, you can ask them to thank *their* friends, too. This is because we owe our happiness not only to ourselves, but also – if not especially – to the people around us. Researchers Fowler (University of California) and Christakis (Harvard Medical School) followed a group of nearly 5,000 people over a span of 20 years; they were able to demonstrate that experiencing happiness is a collective good that spreads through social networks (see Figure 1).[2]

The spread of happiness within a network can be measured up to three degrees of separation. This means that the happiness of one person leads to a chain reaction that not only benefits the individual's immediate friends, but also the friends of their friends, and then the friends of those friends, too. When you have a friend who is happy, your chance of becoming happy increases by 25 per cent. This 'contagion' not only applies to happiness but also to depression, anxiety, loneliness, drinking, eating, and exercise. For example, Fowler and Christakis have shown that if your friends quit smoking, it will also be easier for you to quit smoking as well.

Rose McDermott (Brown University) shows in her collaborative research with Fowler and Christakis that divorce, too, can be contagious.[3] She concludes that when close friends of yours divorce, you will be 33 per cent more likely to leave your partner yourself. The quality of your friends' relationships influences – either positively or negatively – the duration of your own relationship.

Leadership and emotional contagion

Emotions and behaviours can therefore be said to be contagious. If we extend this phenomenon/theory to the influence of the behaviour and leadership styles of leaders, we can see that leaders play an important role in regulating the emotions of their employees and thus the social context of organizations.[4] It is very important to be aware of this as a professional.

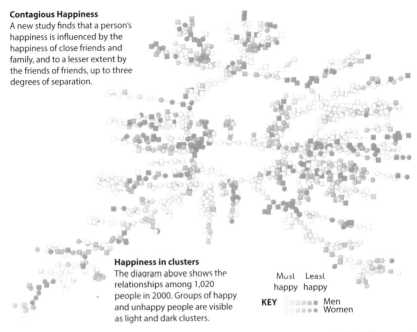

Contagious Happiness
A new study finds that a person's happiness is influenced by the happiness of close friends and family, and to a lesser extent by the friends of friends, up to three degrees of separation.

Happiness in clusters
The diagram above shows the relationships among 1,020 people in 2000. Groups of happy and unhappy people are visible as light and dark clusters.

Most happy   Least happy
KEY ▪▪▪▪▪ Men
         ○○○○○ Women

Sources: James H. Fowler; Nicholas A. Christakis; BMJ

THE NEW YORK TIMES

Figure 1: The dynamic distribution of happiness according to the research of Fowler and Christakis (1983–2003). Each node represents a person: the circles are the women, the squares are the men, and the lines represent their relationships. The lighter the node, the more positive is the individual's experience of happiness; the darker the node, the more negative the individual's experience of happiness. (Source: *New York Times*, 2008)

What does this mean for you and your environment? How do your moods influence your team, and your colleagues?

The idea that you are a good leader merely because you have good employees is not, in itself, illogical. To make this personal to you, allow me to invite you to ask yourself some self-reflective questions:

− Think back to the best supervisor and worst supervisor you have had and ask yourself: 'What did this person mean to me?', 'How did I feel when I was working under their supervision?', and 'What did this person mean to me when I thought about my own development?'
− Similarly, ask yourself questions from the contrary perspective: 'How did the worst supervisor affect me?', 'What mood and performance did this supervisor set and cultivate for me and the team in which I worked?'

If you start to think about the answers to these questions, you will notice that what you find important and what you expect from a supervisor influences the way you assess them and, indeed, the organization as a whole. It will also become clear to you that the 'contagion' of the dynamics between you and your manager went further than you initially thought. Indeed, 'because of the manager' is among the top three stated reasons given in exit interviews as to why employees leave their organization. This is something that should make us think.

Professional contagion on four levels

We can describe professional contagion within organizations on four levels (see Figure 2): the first level is that of **reputation**, the second level that of **first acquaintance**, the third level that of **mutual exchange** of information, and the fourth level that of **reciprocal trust**.

It is important that we, as professionals and leaders, are aware that the contagion of our daily actions extends beyond the direct contact we have with one another, and that we know how to manage this in a positive way.

Reputation	Others know you, but you have never met: – Known by (social) media, organization, or a common acquaintance. – Separated by geography, role, or organizational level.
First acquaintance	The first acquaintance with one another: – Interactions are superficial. – Conversation is not deep or personal. – Trying to find common ground.
Mutual exchange	You maintain regular contact: – Interactions are transactional; consultations take place for mutual benefit. – Emotional investment is conditional. – Most communication comprises facts, ideas, and assessments
Reciprocal Trust	You have regular contact and there is reciprocal trust: – Relationship is built on the basis of consistent behavioural patterns. – Interaction between two people is a mutual investment based on genuine interest. – Reciprocal sharing of feelings and emotions.

Figure 2: Four levels of emotional contagion.

I will now briefly explain the four levels:

1. Our **reputation** may precede us, but we can nevertheless still have a positive influence on it. We see that people in public functions often seek advice and guidance in this regard. So-called spin doctors do their best to ensure that other people mainly or only see the good side of certain individuals. This can be compared to showing the 'good' side of your face when a picture is being taken – much like actor Robert Redford consciously did whenever he was photographed. What people already know about a person, group, or organization determines the selection of new information they take in. By keeping the focus on positive common values and goals of your organization, and by endorsing these values and goals, you can ensure that you do not go along with possible negative currents in unexpected personal conversations. Expressing negative personal feelings can have a major effect on the general perception of your image. Think of a spontaneous conversation that might arise between you and an acquaintance if you meet at a store at the weekend and they ask: 'Are you okay?' The tendency might be to immediately tell them what is on your mind and to 'air your dirty laundry'. However, you should realize what this negative contagion can do to the image of you and your organization.

2. With the **first acquaintance**, we often quickly know whether something feels right or not. Application procedures are a good example of this knowledge. The first thirty seconds after meeting a new person can often make or break an image, even if you carefully prepare yourself before the applicant arrives so that you look and listen objectively, with the help of nice-looking statistical models and communication training. If someone does something that amazes you or that positively surprises you at first glance or when first shaking your hand, the tone can be set for the rest of your conversation. It is important that you are aware of such a 'bias', and that following the moment in which you draw a conclusion that you continue to ask yourself further questions. You may be wrong or find that you have already climbed the 'ladder of inference' (see the interesting work by Chris Argyris[5] on this subject). We already draw conclusions from short impressions and supposed patterns that we recognize from past experiences. Additionally, it is important that we avoid uncomfortable subjects or humour in this first meeting; for example, when you, as a school leader, meet the parents of a new student for the first time. Sometimes well-meaning jokes can come across in an unintended or awkward way, with all the negative consequences this might entail. Remember, a negative first impression cannot easily be remedied or restored.

3. The level of **mutual exchange** is perhaps the most intensive. We are all part of a learning team, a project team, or a sports team; accordingly, we have to achieve something together. When in regular contact with other people, we have to be aware of the energy we transfer. Are you working towards a common ground? Do you share information with one another? Do you comment on your perceptions and how you see things? During this phase, providing honest feedback is necessary, but you must also be open to feedback from other people. Be aware that a major pitfall exists at this level: thinking that all matters and meanings are commonly understood and shared and that, therefore 'they are clear to everyone'. It is essential to continuously communicate with one another about the why, the what, and the how.

4. Finally, there is the fourth level; that of **reciprocal trust**. We can only reach this level if we have gone through the previous levels successfully, and if we are also able – and have the desire – to deepen our relationship with one another. At this level we also show our personal interest in one another and ensure that we quickly resolve any ambiguities. Giving each other a lot of reinforcing feedback (also see Chapter 6) ensures con-tinuous positive development within our respective relationships. The 'maintenance' of a relationship is also essential here; every relationship needs to be maintained, as nothing can continue forever unaided.

These four levels are important for the evaluation of your daily actions. Remember, your actions as well as your verbal and non-verbal behaviour have a direct effect on everyone with whom you interact. The energy you radiate and the way in which you are emotionally connected to your work – as well as to your organization as a whole – forms the basis for building a culture involving a shared vision and common goals. While a majority of organizations and their leaders claim they are aware of such connections, their focus nevertheless remains on the knowledge, skills, and capabilities of their *employees*, such as how they should be behaving in regard to the organizations customers, processes, and innovations etc. This is also called the cognitive culture of an organization. An organization's cognitive culture is of undeniably importance, as it often determines the organization's com-petitiveness and competitive advantages as compared with those of other organizations. This does not wholly determine the sustainable success of an organization, however.

It is at least as important to evaluate and map how people within the organization relate to one another, and how they express such relations – both inside and outside the organization. Indeed, we can clearly see when an emotional culture is not being properly managed and maintained; for example, when unexpected crises occur, such as the COVID-19 crisis, we immediately become aware of any lack or privation regarding proper management and maintenance. Think of employees in the healthcare sector: empathy and persistent kindness are essential, but worker outflow remains a significant issue, particularly as a result of the way in which work is organized and valued in conjunction with the emphasis of 'doing more in less time'. A further example can be seen in education. Every day, educators are challenged with guiding all students through the learning process. However, teachers experience insufficient recognition for fulfilling such important and complex professional roles. Another example is found in organizations in which safety is paramount – such as the police, community support/service officers (CSOs), or those working in the emergency services – and where employees can experience aggression first hand. How do these people deal with their emotions and the resulting contagion of what we should and should not consider to be 'normal'? Furthermore, what does this mean for the continuity of these essential service providers within society itself?

Regardless of this, the expression of our emotions is nevertheless increasingly shifting from non-verbal (passive) to verbal (active) forms. The protest actions of ambulance personnel due to their ongoing confrontations with violence, the yellow vests movement, anti-5G activists, demonstrations related to COVID-19 (COVIDSafe app, emergency laws concerning face masks, etc.), and youths attacking CSOs who are simply doing their job; these are serious signals in our society.

The balance between cognition and emotional engagement

Achieving organizational goals is a complex and holistic process: it involves searching for the right balance between cognition – that is, knowledge and skills – and emotional engagement. Employees must understand how they should behave within their respective fields and roles, based on their knowledge of their profession, and should also understand how such knowledge should be applied within their particular organizations. That employees know and experience *why* such applications are so important and meaningful is itself significant; what is more, employees must be able and willing to commit themselves fully to this task. Every professional has the responsibility to implement this, while it is the responsibility of the management to facilitate the culture and make it possible.

Leadership is challenged and utilized at every level if professionals are invited to function as part of a 'learning team'. In order to make this possible, the leader must undertake the correct steps using their leadership and, in doing so, create a culture of trust that makes such teamwork possible.

In their research, Barsade and O'Neill (2016) analysed the influence of emotional culture within organizations.[6] They concluded that emotional culture has a major influence on, among other things, employee satisfaction, burnout, absenteeism, teamwork and collaboration, and financial results. Positive emotions within organizations are related to better performance, quality, and customer focus; comparatively, negative emotions are associated with anger, sadness, and fear, resulting in performance deterioration and higher employee turnover.

The best leaders are loved and feared, but because it is difficult to unite both in one person, the next best option is to be feared as a leader.
– Niccolò Machiavelli (1469–1527)

Over time, we see interesting shifts in evaluating the importance of this emotional culture and the way leaders consciously use contagion for the success of their organization. While it still may have been a good option for a leader to be feared in Machiavelli's time, today we see that certain other characteristics – such as being clear – are especially appreciated. An example of a leader who currently ranks high on the 'sincere and loved' metric is New Zealand's Prime Minister, Jacinda Ardern, who received the highest score ever in the poll by market-research firm Reid Research in May 2020.

Show your warmth before showing your competence

Behavioural scientists Fiske et al. (2002) indicate that, when assessing leaders, we primarily focus on two characteristics.[7] On the one hand, we focus on how warm, reliable, and relationship-oriented the leader is; on the other hand, we focus on how competent, terrifying, and powerful that leader is. Based on these qualities, employees then estimate their manager's character and intentions.

When we form an image of another individual, we evaluate several of their qualities to arrive at a coherent and complete image of that person. However, the aforementioned characteristics of warmth and competence comprise more than 90 per cent of the (positive or negative) impressions we form of the people around us.

		Competence	
		Low	High
Warmth	High	**Paternalistic** *Low status, not competitive* *(housemothers/fathers, elderly* *people, etc.)*	**Admiration** *High status, not competitive* *(allies, relationships, etc.)*
	Low	**Contemptuous** *Low status, competitive* *(poor people, addicts, etc.)*	**Envious** *High status, competitive* *(very wealthy people, fast-* *emerging competitors in the field,* *etc.)*

Figure 3: The Stereotype Content Model and the subdivision of competence and warmth into four scenarios.

These two dimensions are described in a study by Fiske et al. (2002) according to the so-called *Stereotype Content Model (SCM)* (see Figure 3). In this model we clearly see that the evaluation of what we experience as being 'warm' and 'cold' represents a zeitgeist, one based on the dominance of a certain culture as well as the norms it has built up.

This model has shown its reliability across various national and international samples and has provided consistent results from repeated measurements taken by the same researchers using the same instrument. Accordingly, the SCM is able to predict affective responses for different groups, regardless of their cultural differences. The model is also supported by empirical evidence in areas such as interpersonal perception. Interpersonal perception is based on our evolutionary predisposition to judge strangers, first according to the warmth dimension and, subsequently, according to the competence dimension. Warmth in this model is about our ability to trust one another; when we judge someone as warm, we often see 'the other' as friendly, reliable, moral, and empathetic.

Competence in this model concerns how capable someone is in carrying out their intentions; when we judge someone to be competent, we often see them as intelligent, decisive, and skilled. It is interesting that a person's competence will only be assessed after their characteristics have been evaluated according to the warmth dimension. Dimensional combinations generated as a result of warmth and competence result in four stereotypical assessments (see box below).

Four stereotypical assessments
The first scenario concerns someone who is rated high on competence but low on warmth (the **envious stereotype,** according to the scheme). This person often appears cold and unfriendly to others, but at the same time evokes admi-

ration because they are extremely competent. Others resent them, due to their competence, and so we are left envious. This evaluation assessment, which follows a judgment after only a quick evaluation, is often used in regard to affluent people, or fellow professionals or competitors in the field.

The second scenario is the exact opposite of the first: in this situation, a person is judged as having low competence but as being very warm (the **paternalistic stereotype**). This person often comes across as friendly, reliable, and sincere; their lack of competence is generally not seen as a negative trait, but does evoke a sense of compassion in some other people, especially those who feel superior in regard to their own competence. Think of this stereotype as employees who are marginalized because they are about to retire, or 'stay-at-home mothers and fathers' who are underappreciated.

The third scenario is when we classify someone as inferior; judging them low on the warmth dimension and low on the competence dimension (the **contemptuous stereotype**). People often look down on these people and are contemptuous of them. This stereotypical assessment is often used for drug addicts, people who have 'failed at life'.

Machiavelli described the best leader as a person who is both loved and feared; unfortunately, this combination is not a common one. (Therefore, according to Machiavelli, the next best option for leader is for them to be feared.) Sometimes, this is referred to as the so-called halo effect (see also Chapter 2), where attributing a very positive quality suggests that other qualities are also present. This is the final scenario, wherein a person scores high on both competence and warmth (**admiration stereotype**). These people are often admired by us, and we accord them this talent due to the fact that they appear to us as being nice and reliable. Furthermore, they pose no threat to us. This evaluation assessment is usually given to those people who are closest to us.

It is important to emphasize that humans like to use heuristics and form stereotypes. The image employees have of their manager(s) is the truth to that employee at that moment in time, and this subjective truth ultimately influences their behaviour and performance. Leadership behaviour is undeniably contagious!

Is it better to be loved or to be competent as a leader?

A majority of individuals work hard in order to demonstrate their competencies because they want to appear both strong and skilled. Unfortunately, this approach is insufficiently effective within leadership. If leaders demonstrate their skills and strengths before they gain the confidence of their employees, they risk creating a culture of fear, thereby provoking dysfunctional behaviour among those workers they are trying to lead. It is important that the leader behaves in a morally correct manner; an amoral leader threatens the group as a whole because their behaviour is unpredictable.

Researchers Mayer et al. (2009)[8] have studied the trickle-down effect of moral leadership. Moral leadership means that you are aware of those core values that are important to you and that you act with awareness according to these values. This includes and concerns specific values, namely what is 'good' and what is 'bad'.

This study shows contagion from leaders occurs in this situation. Senior leaders who behave morally positively affect the moral behaviour of middle managers just as, subsequently, middle managers have a positive effect on the behaviour of their employees. In the research itself, these employees demonstrated greater commitment, undertook more tasks than were demanded of them according to their job description, and were extremely motivated towards achieving organizational goals.

Despite this, it is still generally believed that someone can be an effective leader without being loved. While this may technically be true, the chances of achieving high effectiveness while not being loved are very slim. In a study by Zenger and Folkman[9] using more than 50,000 leaders, only 27 scored high on the 'very competent' metric but not on the 'loved' metric, meaning that the odds of being an effective but unloved leader are roughly 1 in 2,000.

It is therefore imperative to be competent as a leader but, in its behaviour and in all of its other expressions – including verbal and non-verbal expressions – leadership must be sincere, warm, and moral.

Leadership and your transition

Supported by the research and opinions of scientists, philosophers, and top leaders and professionals, we now stand on the precipice of abandoning classic management theories and redefining leadership as a dynamic between people, one that is focused on achieving a certain goal. In fact, as shall be seen later, this redefined leadership is focused on achieving an evolutionary goal – a goal that an organization naturally moves towards. The change and movement we are instigating here comes from a focus on total planning and control, as well as moving towards continuous learning and (re)discovery and re-evaluation together. This book reveals and presents several insights into the different theories of leadership and leadership development, the impact this has on people within organizations, and the impact this has on organizations as a whole. I challenge all of you to make your own evaluation.

My question to you is as follows: How will you shape the transition in your leadership and create your impact? I invite you to ask yourself this question in each and every chapter, and undertake your choices and actions accordingly.

Chapter 1 provides a brief description of where we come from in regard to thinking about leadership, as well as where we are today. Is it possible to learn and develop leadership further? What does research into this process reveal? I can already disclose the following: there is positive news for us all, we can learn far more than we might think would be possible. You will come to discover how this learning works and what it can mean for you.

Chapter 2 shows that focusing on strengths is many times more impactful than focusing on weaknesses if you want to achieve your goals as a leader and as a professional. Why and how you should do this is explained using the so-called CPO-model.

In **Chapter 3** I discuss the quest for success, as described and investigated by many different leadership gurus. What are the themes of this quest and how can various research studies be used to help us to get a grip on the behaviours leading to greater and higher success?

Chapter 4 explains that, ultimately, the connection between us and those with whom we work – that is, our team – is a crucial factor in achieving objectives. We take a look at making an emotional connection: how does this work and what does it yield for your organization?

Chapter 5 focuses on organizational transformation. After seeing that we can and should do things differently when working together, how should we go about achieving this? What change is most urgently needed? How can I direct change in a positive way? Your leadership is decisive in regard to the culture of your organization and, therefore, the ability to organize and achieve organizational transformation. This transformation begins with your development as a leader; not *they*, but *we* have to change; accordingly, *I* have to change as a leader

Chapter 6 looks at feedback, and makes it clear to us that we will only be able to change and improve if we maintain a constant dialogue with one another. Giving feedback to one another and inviting each other to upkeep feedback communication is the most important intervention for creating a sustainable existence for both people and organizations. However, we also find that both giving and receiving feedback is very difficult. Unfortunately, we find that people often do not deal with feedback in the right way. To help you to understand the fear associated with feedback, I will take you through the workings of our psychological needs and provide you with the concrete tools so that you can deal with this process in a good and positive way.

Chapter 7 provides us with a broader insight into how we can learn from one another if we see things through the eyes of different generations. As a representative of 'Generation X', my interest in this theme was piqued during the 1990s. The introduction of generation management itself is a plea to facilitate sustainable employability that promotes harmony between the various generations. An overview of the different generations present in the workplace, as well as the impact and the needs of these generations – with a particular focus on the behaviour of the newest generation of leaders, Generation Y – provides an up-to-date picture, a picture that we can use as a basis for our own interactions with individuals from different generations than our own.

Chapter 8 focuses on leadership practice from the perspective of the male–female dichotomy. in 1949, Simone de Beauvoir wrote: 'I hesitated for a long time to write a book about women. It is an annoying topic, and what's more, it's not new. So much ink has already been wasted around the squabbling of feminism'. She goes on to say: 'It would never occur to a man to write a book about the special position that men occupy'. As a woman, an entrepreneur, and a consultant I have, over the past 33 years, experienced how images of men and women give direction – generally unconsciously, though sometimes also consciously – to certain choices. Keeping in mind the challenge of getting the most out of every professional, this chapter considers the current position of women in the workforce based on current data. We ask the question: What images do we have of women in regard to their roles as leaders and how, throughout our own transition, can we put people of all genders in the spotlight so they thrive in the pursuit of greater impact?

A diverse society needs inclusive leadership, and inclusion has itself become a mission for all organizations within today's society. Accordingly, **Chapter 9** discusses inclusion and diversity, as well as how we can structure our leadership in order to achieve positive exchanges among people of different backgrounds. Organizing a safe climate and fair treatment is a moral task, and it is perhaps on this particular theme that leadership continues to have its greatest impact. How can you yourself facilitate this? I hereby invite you to take another good look in the mirror.

Chapter 10 comprises the 10th step in your personal-development approach. Here you take a critical look at the conclusions we have drawn from the various themes in the book, undertaking your own choices in order to make a difference using your own strengths and passions: You direct your impact.

The timeline presented at the beginning of this book provides an overview of thinkers, doers, and researchers who have contributed to current views and strategies that enable us as leaders – along with our employees, and for our organizations – to undertake more successful interventions. Statements by these individuals are included throughout this book as quotes. We see that our current views have deep roots based on long histories, and that many of the ideas and views concerning the necessary transition of our leadership have been discussed and expressed by philosophers and researchers in the past already.

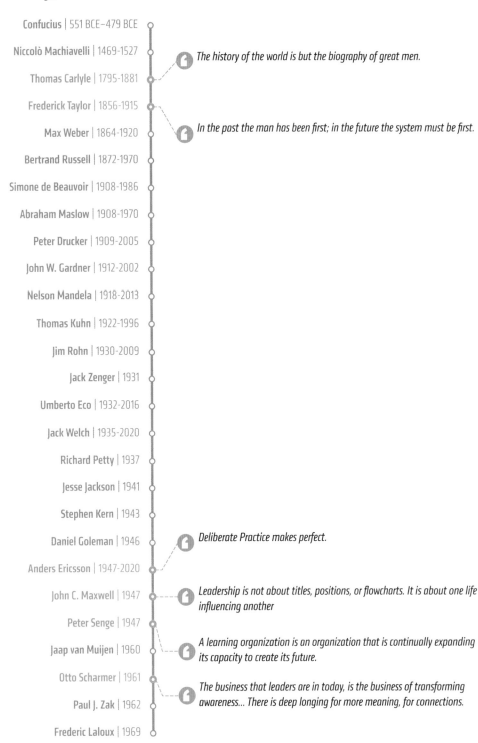

Confucius | 551 BCE–479 BCE

Niccolò Machiavelli | 1469-1527

Thomas Carlyle | 1795-1881

The history of the world is but the biography of great men.

Frederick Taylor | 1856-1915

Max Weber | 1864-1920

In the past the man has been first; in the future the system must be first.

Bertrand Russell | 1872-1970

Simone de Beauvoir | 1908-1986

Abraham Maslow | 1908-1970

Peter Drucker | 1909-2005

John W. Gardner | 1912-2002

Nelson Mandela | 1918-2013

Thomas Kuhn | 1922-1996

Jim Rohn | 1930-2009

Jack Zenger | 1931

Umberto Eco | 1932-2016

Jack Welch | 1935-2020

Richard Petty | 1937

Jesse Jackson | 1941

Stephen Kern | 1943

Daniel Goleman | 1946

Deliberate Practice makes perfect.

Anders Ericsson | 1947-2020

John C. Maxwell | 1947

Leadership is not about titles, positions, or flowcharts. It is about one life influencing another

Peter Senge | 1947

Jaap van Muijen | 1960

A learning organization is an organization that is continually expanding its capacity to create its future.

Otto Scharmer | 1961

Paul J. Zak | 1962

The business that leaders are in today, is the business of transforming awareness... There is deep longing for more meaning, for connections.

Frederic Laloux | 1969

1.   Leadership

The history of the world is but the biography of great men.
– Thomas Carlyle (1795–1881), Scottish writer and historian

What distinguishes highly successful people from less successful ones? Whether in the field of sports, science, or business, every person has the ability to recognize exceptional achievements in others, as well as the ability to measure themselves according to these exceptional standards. If we are confronted with a group of top performers, we might often be envious and potentially perceive their 'talent' with jealousy. Top performance is often attributed to innate qualities: 'These individuals are gifted with a talent that not "everyone" has', is a sentiment that is often thought (and vocalized). Furthermore, when we think of great leaders in history, we are often confronted with unconscious assumptions – formed by philosophers, and social and religious beliefs – about these individuals. Recurring questions concerning this subject include 'Are great leaders born or formed?', and 'Can leadership be taught and developed, or is it innate?' Such questions arise from the well-known discussion of *nature versus nurture*.

There are many definitions of leadership, as well as many theories about leadership, leadership styles, and leadership traits.

– The **trait theory** states that successful leaders have certain innate qualities that distinguish them from everyone else. This theory emphasizes personal characteristics and does not account for situations in which behaviours are to be applied. Various studies were conducted throughout the 1960s that investigated this very subject, although these studies yielded contradictory results. Ultimately, however, five basic elements have endured within the discussion and discourse, and these have been confirmed and reconfirmed by several studies. These elements have become popularly known as the Big Five, and include neuroticism versus stability, extraversion versus introversion, openness versus closedness, conscientiousness versus laxity, and friendliness versus antagonism.[10]
– In contrast to the trait theory is the **classical conditioning theory**: this theory emphasizes behaviour, something that is learnable. When leadership behaviour is learned, it can be applied to any given situation.
– The **contingency theory** states that there is no universal leadership style, that leadership depends on context, and that behaviour must be adapted to specific situations.[11] Accordingly, something that may

be successful in a certain context may not be successful in another context. According to this theory, not all great leaders from the past may have proven to be so successful today or in a different age or zeitgeist. For example, questions are often raised as to why some controversial historical leaders had such a significant impact, and why they were so successful in their own time.

– Finally, there is the **charismatic and transformational theory**, whereby leaders are committed to taking people to higher goals and levels of achievement. The work of psychologist Bernard M. Bass (1985) provides an explanation of the psychological mechanisms of transformation and a means to measure leaders' influence on their adherents.[12]

One of the best-known theories in this field historically is the *Great Man theory*.[13] This theory assumes that leadership qualities are intrinsic: that is, that great leaders are born, not formed. The theory has its origins in the nineteenth century, and was made especially popular by the Scottish author Thomas Carlyle, who stated that the structure and form of our history has been determined entirely by an exceptional group of charismatic leaders.[14] Everything historically achieved in this world has resulted from the thoughts, behaviours, and aims of great leaders.

The *Great Man theory* received sharp criticism from several people, including the British sociologist Herbert Spencer (1820–1903).[15] According to Spencer, it is an absurd and ungrounded scientific notion to reduce historical events to merely a few great leaders; rather, it was the societies around these people that made it possible for them to become great. Although the *Great Man theory* is now considered to be obsolete, it nevertheless remains popular. This is simultaneously fascinating and disturbing. The idea that the most effective leaders have similar (innate) personality traits has many implications for thinking about leadership, as well as the means by which people can come to positions of leadership and fulfil their roles therein. Negative answers are still given to questions such as 'Does leadership development make sense?' and 'Is excellent leadership for everyone?' The means by which the potential within organizations (i.e. opportunities available to employees) is positioned and exploited is partly determined by these thoughts (see also Chapters 8 and 9).

Returning to the 'Is excellent leadership for everyone?' question, the answer is, happily, a resounding 'Yes'. When analysing how peak performance is achieved, we must forget myths about innate talent. Every one of us who is born with a healthy brain has the capacity for self-development and the

Figure 1.1: Taylorism: mass production according to piece work. (Source: Wikipedia)

ability to deliver exceptional performance. However, the most effective way to do this for yourself and your environment is via a personal journey of development. Remember: your impact and the positive effect you have on other people starts with yourself.

Let us explore the playing field in greater detail: 'What are our ideas of leadership?', 'How does leadership work?', 'How do we see and assess successful leadership?', and 'What is our paradigm?'

A paradigm shift

> *In the past the man has been first; in the future the system must be first.*
> – Frederick Taylor (1856–1915), American mechanical engineer

Through what is now known as *Taylorism*, Frederick Taylor made an important contribution to the theory of scientific management (see Figure 1.1).[16] In light of Taylor's investigation into a new form of business management, research was conducted on how people work on various tasks, with new processes being introduced as a result of data collection and the application of mathematical models. This was not done through *trial and error,* but rather through evidence-informed data.

It is important that the background of this movement is properly understood. While the second industrial revolution made mass production possible, this innovation also brought about many administrative problems. Taylor wished to contribute to a solution to these problems and can therefore be seen as one of the first business consultants. During Taylor's time people had to be motivated to undertake simple work. According to Taylor, this was best achieved through extrinsic motivation, and so employees were paid according to the 'piece wages' system (i.e. per action or product made); the more pieces a worker made, the more they earned. This means of rewarding workers is still used in organizations today. For example, think of bonus culture today, which has been repeatedly reintroduced despite numerous recessions and crises. Taylorian work, however, was mainly concerned with simple and often repetitive work, however, and it must be remembered that Taylorian work originated under a different zeitgeist.

Today, our organizations operate under a flatter – and more complex – organizational hierarchy. Environments are rapidly changing, as are the interests of customers, partners, investors, and regulators. The younger generation is more highly educated today than it was in the past, with individuals consciously choosing to enter certain professions and a certain roles. Consequently, the battle for 'talent' is increasingly felt within the labour market. For instance, shortages of healthcare staff and teachers are becoming increasingly urgent in society. In addition, increasing digitization generates a demand for competent but also innovative employees who are not motivated solely by extrinsic rewards. Accordingly, Taylor's method is no longer efficient nor effective in the present day, while organizations operating as basic hierarchical machines are no longer able to survive. The 'organizations as machines' paradigm has shifted into a new paradigm, one of 'organizations as organisms'. Organizations in this new paradigm are described as being nimble, flexible, and *agile.*

Agility refers to an organization's ability to consistently adapt without having to change its overall approach.

Agile organizations can act quickly and decisively, and are able to constantly adapt to new circumstances. McKinsey's report *The Five Trademarks of Agile Organizations* (January 2018) describes the characteristics of such agile organizations. According to McKinsey, the development from machine-driven organizations towards organizations as organisms is concerned with

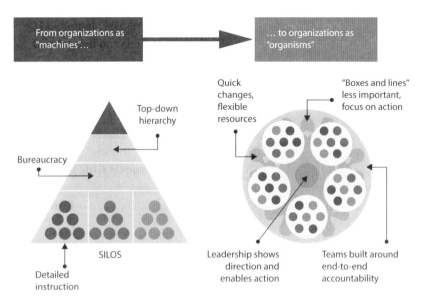

Figure 1.2: The development from machine-driven organizations to organizations as an organism. (Source: Aghina et al., 2018)

redefining strategy, structure, people, processes, and technology. Figure 1.2 shows the development from the old paradigm to the new paradigm.

According to the new paradigm, organizations are increasingly seen as living things that have their own sense of direction. Instead of trying to predict and control the future from the top down, everyone in the organization is invited to examine – from the perspective of their own role and position – the organization's goals and what those in the organization want it to become. The book *Reinventing Organizations* by Frederic Laloux[17] provides an overview of the different trends of thought pertaining to organizations and leadership over the centuries. Based on Ken Wilber's[18] theory of evolution, Laloux distinguishes five types of organizations – giving each their own identifying colour – according to their respective zeitgeists and the breakthroughs they managed to realize in their own times (see Figure 1.3).

Concerning our own time, Laloux advocates for organizations to be led in greater accordance with nature, whereby no individual is in charge. He asserts that the time of *command and control* is over, and that now is a time of *sensing and responding*. There is a balance here between predictability and flexibility. According to Laloux, people living during the era of so-called 'teal'-coloured organizations actively organize themselves around an evolutionary goal, one that is constantly evolving. This goal gives the

Type of organization	Most important breakthroughs	Leadership style
Impulsive (red)	**Division of labour** **Authority/boss**	Hunting/actively chasing
Compliant (amber)	**Formal roles** (Stable and scalable hierarchies) **Processes** (Long-term perspectives)	Paternalistic–authoritative (restricting freedom and autonomy)
Competitive (orange)	**Innovation** **Accountability** **Meritocracy**	Goal- and task-oriented Decisive
Pluralistic (green)	Empowerment A value-driven culture Stakeholder model	Consensus-oriented Participating and servicing
Evolutionary (teal)	Self-management Wholeness Evolutionary/purpose	Shared leadership, with inner justice and purpose as primary motivator

Figure 1.3: The five types of organizations according to Laloux

organization its right to exist and is concerned with the value it adds to the world. This process is iterative, and it is a process whereby all members of an organization actively listen in regard to the organization's purpose in the world, acting upon this accordingly. I will expound the significance of teal-coloured organizations with a view to creating an engaged team in Chapter 4.

Learning organizations

> *A learning organization is an organization that is continually expanding its*
> *capacity to create its future.*
> – Peter Senge (1947), American scientist

Hitherto, the twenty-first century has been characterized by a focus on continuous change and innovation, something that has resulted in increased competition between companies and institutions. Organizations must continuously improve if they are to be able to adapt to customer wishes: for example, by providing online lessons, utilizing other forms of communication, or designing the building in which they operate in a different way. Furthermore, leaders are tasked with including employees in these developments.

The bad news is that many initiatives for change end up failing. Indeed, it turns out that sustainably changing newly defined principles for processes, activities, and behaviours is an extremely difficult goal for organizations to implement. In referring to things such as quasi-standard solutions – for example, IT tools and methods that are necessary in order to support or even lead a change – Laloux states in his book that: 'The realization is there that we can no longer continue like this'. For example, rolling out the use of computers or tablets in schools does not automatically lead to change. On the contrary, such a process demands that another educational improvement and/or change is needed. Such complex challenges mean that organizations and their people must relate to one another differently than was the case in the past. It is important that both the organization (including the organization's management, board, and leaders) as well as those people who work for that organization understand the ultimate goal towards which they are growing together and that, furthermore, they have the right knowledge to achieve this goal.

Through their research into organizational change and leadership development, Peter Senge and Otto Scharmer provide great insights into how organizations can develop and adapt. Based on his research, Peter Senge, an organizational change specialist and author of the book *The Fifth Discipline*, has unearthed ground-breaking information about organizational change and how we act as leaders and employees.[19] According to Senge, the main challenge is that change is not just implemented by the leader but rather by everyone within the organization. For this, it is necessary for *everyone* within the organization to be included in the organization's changes, and that they are given the opportunity to develop themselves as well. Therefore, we must also think differently about the role of leadership itself as it exists within organizations.

> *The business that leaders are in today, is the business of transforming awareness ...*
> *There is deep longing for more meaning, for connections.*
> – Otto Scharmer (1961), professor at the Massachusetts Institute of
> Technology (MIT)

With Senge's work in mind, we need to understand that leadership development must concern the development of everyone within an organization. Otto Scharmer, the founder of the so-called *Theory U*, states that so-called classic leadership development programmes – in which we train people to show and/or improve certain behaviour – are not successful in bringing about organizational change.[20] In order to be successful, value must be attached to both individual and organizational development. Leadership development is a process in which employees and leaders intertwine; a natural connection and interaction takes place. Organizational change is a common good; it benefits everyone within the organization but also requires everyone to make a contribution.

In conclusion, we can say that leadership development is a strategic necessity, not only for the leaders of an organization but also for the organization as a whole. Leadership development is the core that facilitates and enables the overall development of an organization. The definition of leadership I would like to introduce at this point is:

> *Leadership is the behaviour that elevates individual performance and drives superior organizational outcomes.*

Is development possible?

Ways of thinking about how people in an organization should and can interact, and how goals can be achieved, have gradually changed over time. Working collaboratively across every layer of the organization is necessary for change. Using their own developmental process, professionals can contribute to the common course of an organization, as well as to the development of other people within that organization. This means a different vision of leadership, as well as a different way by which formal leaders position themselves and open themselves up to their environments.

The methods by which, for example, people are considered as belonging to a certain type – after which their strengths are used accordingly – provide more and more material for deliberation and discussion regarding whether this leads to sustainable change. The idea that people can undergo a fundamental change is generally met with some resistance. The often-abused modes in management courses and professionalization activities are: 'That's just the way I am', or 'That is in my character and people's characters cannot be changed'. While it may be hard to believe, people can actually change. For example, it can be deduced from the research done by Jack Zenger and Joe Folkman that effective leadership does not depend on a number of fixed character traits; rather, it starts with becoming aware of what works for you and what you want to become better at.

> **How you can make a difference**
> In this book I refer, among other things, to the data collected all over the world by Jack Zenger and Joe Folkman and their partners.[21] Their ground-breaking work, as described in *The Extraordinary Leader*, *The New Extraordinary Leader*, and *How to be Exceptional*, provides clear insights into how leaders and professionals

can make a difference for organizations. Zenger and Folkman's studies now include over 1.5 million data points across more than 120,000 leaders worldwide. A number of interesting elements have emerged from this research that have had a drastic effect on thinking about leadership and leadership development. The data used herein were acquired from a highly valid 360-degree feedback instrument developed by Zenger and Folkman themselves. Analyses of these data were then utilized to compare leaders in different sectors worldwide, and also to share case studies on the effects of development on organizations. Academica BV – an institution that I lead, and which also provides higher education and conducts research – used Zenger and Folkman's research approach to collect data from various organizations in the Netherlands. In this book I share a number of analyses of these international data as well as the data of educational institutions in the Netherlands, as acquired and analysed by Academica.

> *Deliberate Practice makes perfect.*
> – Anders Ericsson (1947–2020), Swedish psychologist, professor of psychology at Florida State University

Revolutionary insights into what we generally call talent development have been given to us through the work of Anders Ericsson, a psychologist specializing in human performance and expertise.[22] His latest book, *Piek*, which he co-authored with Robert Pool, answers the question of how ordinary people are able to achieve extraordinary achievements. One interesting example from this book is the Hungarian couple László and Klara Polgár, who wished to demonstrate that anything can be learned (see box below).

The art of chess

Thirty years ago, Hungarian education leaders László and Klara Polgár decided to challenge the popular assumption that women are not as good as men when it comes to spatial skills. Every day they decided to systematically teach their three daughters the art of chess in order to make a point about the power of education. They provided their daughters with the correct training materials before teaching them to play chess.

Their goal was to demonstrate the power of education, but education alone was insufficient for them to achieve the goal. Through coaching, setting challenging goals, and encouragement, the Polgárs' daughters continued to develop and improve their skills. The outcome was extraordinary: all three daughters became high-level chess players. Today, the youngest daughter, Judit, is one of the best chess players in the world, at some point having beaten almost all her male opponents.

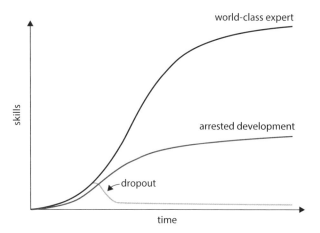

Figure 1.4: Skills development according to Anders Ericsson.
(Source: Ericsson & Pool, 2017)

Intrigued by the question of what makes people experts in a particular discipline, Ericsson has spent years studying individuals who deliver exceptional achievements and who are counted among the topmost world leaders within their particular fields, including chess players, musicians, athletes, and businessmen. Among other things, Ericsson conducted experiments using random people and demonstrated, among other findings, that it is possible to get everyone to remember a sequence of more than ten digits at a time but that, through targeted practice and guidance, people can be taught to remember up to eighty digits. Accordingly, the correct method, guidance, and the right amount of time are all needed in order to achieve excellent performance. Figure 1.4 depicts the three different learning curves that can be distinguished.

We see that the so-called 'drop-out' learning curve is both short and intense, but that it is not sustainable. We are aware of many initiatives whereby people start learning a new skill whereby many soon drop out. For example, I may decide to play golf; all my friends are taking up golf, and so I decide to go to golf classes. Throughout the first few lessons I am still motivated to learn, but soon I notice that my learning golf does not fit in well with my schedule and that, furthermore, I have insufficient time to do everything correctly. Slowly but surely, I start to apologize for me being unable to achieving my golf skills certificate. As a result of this, I decide to quit learning golf.

The second line represents that of stagnating development. Here we see that we can make progress through practice and repetition when learning a skill, but that our level starts to stagnate over time. An example of this can be seen in the good and also ambitious recreational tennis player who has reached a reasonably high level over the years – and who participates in club competitions – but who, ultimately, remains at this level as they do not progress any further. It is not necessary to go any further because, in this scenario, the tennis player is already of a higher level than most people.

Finally, is the line of the expert; this person makes a huge difference in their development through targeted and systemic training and continues to pursue their own improvement. Such an individual is specifically guided to get the most out of their skill. For them, there is always room for improvement, the adage – as we can recognize with top athletes such as Serena Williams and Roger Federer – and the aim is therefore to continuously achieve this through targeted training.

The conclusion that can be drawn from Ericsson's research is that people can deliver exceptional performances assuming that that they take the right approach. There are three preconditions for reaching the top according to this method:

– First of all, you must be committed enough to want to practice. Not merely to practice, but to conduct goal-oriented and systematic practice; Ericsson calls this **deliberate practice**.
– Secondly, you should take enough time to practice and have the right training materials and facilities.
– Finally, you must be able to access the right coaching, guidance, and support.

All people who reach the absolute top of their respective fields have gone through these three steps. The journey to superior performance is anything but an easy one; it requires combativeness, sacrifice, and honest but often painful self-evaluation. According to Ericsson, goal-oriented training is characterized by a number of important properties:

– Purposeful training develops skills that other people already possess and for which effective training techniques already exist.
– It takes place outside of someone's comfort zone.
– It is based on a clearly defined objective and concerns the improvement of some aspect of the intended performance, rather than a vague overall improvement.
– It is purposeful, which means it requires a person's full attention and conscious effort (i.e. focus).
– Commentary on and adjustment of training in response to that commentary is an essential feature of deliberate training.
– It leads to the development of effective mental images.

In 2013, researchers Zenger and Folkman specifically investigated the effect of leaders' commitment and focus on improving their own leadership.[23] They investigated the leadership effectiveness of 545 leaders within three different organizations and, by means of a pre- and post-test, determined whether leadership development was actually effective. The pre-test specifically looked at the profile of leaders with a so-called *fatal flaw* (i.e. a critical short-coming). As measured through Zenger and Folkman's 360-degree feedback, these leaders averaged in the 20th percentile of leadership effectiveness in relation to the other leaders in their database, and these leaders (those with fatal flaws) were therefore perceived as inadequate – after all, 80 per cent of leaders from Zenger and Folkman's database scored higher than these leaders. Subsequently, these leaders worked purposefully on their leadership development through the use of effective coaching, training, and guidance. The results of the post-test were extremely encouraging: the leaders increased in their effectiveness from the 20th percentile to the 51st percentile. The result of this research alone gives us a sound confirmation that we can develop.

However, we must ask ourselves whether the major challenge lies in improving those leaders who are insufficiently effective. There are categories of leaders which represent a larger proportion of the total. Should we not, therefore, merely focus on those leaders who are already just good, and who could increase their impact significantly, as described by Jim Collins (2001) in his book *Good to Great*? This largest cohort of professionals and leaders comprises those individuals who are good, but who cannot yet be considered 'great'. We know that good leaders achieve good results, but how is it that certain leaders are able to achieve better results still? Through the work by Anders Ericsson, we see that far more can be achieved through *deliberate practice* than with ordinary practice. Is it possible to then apply this method specifically to leadership? Results from studies that apply to this context show categorically that the excellent leaders have a significant positive effect on their peers – 'good leaders' – concerning a number of varied organizational results and that, furthermore, this has a subsequent effect on all layers of their organizations. For example, this refers to the impact on achieving organizational goals, employee engagement, and customer satisfaction.

To envisage the effect of leadership development on leaders who are already considered to be 'good', Zenger and Folkman's research also looked at leaders who were without fatal flaws – that is, good leaders. In their study, Zenger and Folkman looked at those good leaders who scored at the top of this cohort, averaging in the 60th percentile of leadership effectiveness. These leaders also proved themselves as able to develop further, improving from a good performance to an excellent performance. From the post-test, Zenger and Folkman saw an increase from an average of 22 percentile points, to an average of the 82nd percentile of leadership effectiveness. With this score, this group now belongs to cohort of 'extraordinary leaders', as Zenger and Folkman call those leaders who belong to the top 20 per cent of leaders in their database. These *extraordinary leaders* are those who have the greatest impact and make a meaningful difference within their organizations. The various research results will be further explained in Chapter 2.

Making Shift Happen

Good leadership is different from excellent leadership, something that organizations and employees are both entitled to! Be assured that this is not about striving for perfection, however, because no one is perfect. Nevertheless, it is important to realize that there will always be expectations that concern your actions and your behaviour; hard work does not necessarily mean that you will have a significant impact. Formal leaders are always in the spotlight, whether they want to be or not, and people expect something from them because of this. Everyone is able to apply greater focus and thus realize a greater impact. If you consciously direct the effect you wish to make, you will be amazed at the outcome.

> *I am careful not to confuse excellence with perfection. Excellence, I can reach for;*
> *perfection is God's business.*
> – Michael J. Fox (1961), Canadian actor

A self-assessment
- What effect does being appreciated have on you?
- What effect does this have on your behaviour?
- What effect does it have on you if you understand and have an insight into how your daily activities contribute to organizational goals?
- What is the effect of your manager motivating or observing you while you also receive targeted and stimulating feedback so that you can do your work with even greater efficacy?

Figure 1.5: The effect of leadership: repeated studies demonstrate the relationship. (Source: Zenger & Folkman, 2012)

As a result of my guidance and my investigations at various organizations over the past 33 years, both in the Netherlands and globally, one thing has been made clear to me: the means by which leaders and professionals commit themselves to their organization and their team has an enormous impact on the success of that organization. The influence of leadership is often many times greater than the person themselves understands. It is therefore important that the following point is made clear: *if I understand how leadership works, I can start to consciously steer it in a positive way.*

According to the new paradigm of agile organizations, the development of leaders is viewed in the context of their effect on their entire organization/ team. We operate together as part of a dynamic process and depend on one another in order to achieve the objectives of our organization.

When we compare leadership effectiveness (obtained through 360-degree feedback) against employee engagement (obtained by asking employees the relevant leaders questions about their engagement), a positive relationship can be seen. For example, the higher a leader's leadership effectiveness is, then the higher their employee engagement score will be. Furthermore, we also see higher employee satisfaction and productivity.

The fact that employee engagement influences many organizational goals, such as customer satisfaction, is not new. We do not only see this effect in large and medium-sized commercial organizations, and it can also be observed in non-profit organizations, such as in educational and healthcare organizations. Leadership has an impact in both a direct and indirect way. Better and more motivated employees are created by better leaders, and these employees have more positive relationships with their customers and clients, thereby achieving better results for their organizations (see Figure 1.5).

Case: The education leader in the Netherlands
The direct and indirect effects of leadership are shown using data on educational leaders, collected, and analysed by Academica.

Over a 6-year period, the effectiveness of 1,150 managers in the Netherlands (administrators, school leaders, and team leaders) in primary education, secondary education, and secondary vocational education was examined using Zenger and Folkman's 360-degree questionnaire. The results of this research are described in detail in the 2018 article *De staat van de Nederlandse onderwijsleider* (The state of the Dutch education leader).[24] A number of basic conclusions can be drawn from the feedback provided within the professional context of education leaders by more than 25,000 respondents:

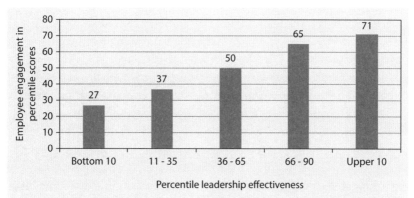

Figure 1.6: The relationship between leadership effectiveness and employee engagement. (Source: Academica Research, 2018)

1. The Dutch leader in education has a direct effect on the engagement of tea-chers and, subsequently, an indirect effect on parental and pupil satisfaction, as well as on the learning efficiency of pupils and students.
2. The school leader's leadership is important for employees and school organi-zations.
3. Leadership is learnable using targeted development and focus. An improve-ment in scores subsequently becomes clear during a second measurement following conscious development and guidance.
4. Here, where leaders at the top of the organization score relatively low on effectiveness, we can see that the formal leaders under them also score lower in this regard. The level of the impact at all levels in the organization is determined by the top.

The leader's impact is immediately reflected in employee engagement. Fi-gure 1.6 shows the relationship between leaders' 360-degree feedback question-naire scores as compared with their employee-engagement scores (which were measured in the study by using a separate questionnaire, to which the leaders' employees gave their respective responses).

For her master's thesis, Kimberly Kwanten further analysed data acquired by Academica, focusing specifically on 154 school leaders and their schools in the primary education sector.[25] Kwanten examined the dynamics between leadership, employee engagement, and school results (i.e. the Cito test scores of the schools of the relevant school leaders). Her research demonstrated the relationship between those scores concerning school leaders' specific leadership behaviours, as well as the engagement scores of teachers in connection with the annual Cito results (the average scores of the central final test of primary educa-tion in the Netherlands). A higher leadership behaviour score was found to lead to a higher level of engagement among employees in the leaders' respective schools; furthermore, these schools were found to have better Cito results than average.

Academica's data also show the effect of these leaders' leadership on the results of students within their respective schools. The data confirm that which most people surrounding these leaders already felt or sensed when entering their school: their leadership is of great influence on the overall performance of the school.

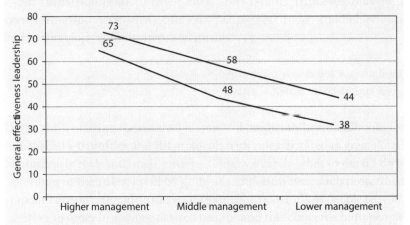

Figure 1.7: The top determines the impact: two school organizations compared. (Source: Academica research, 2019)

> *Leadership is not about titles, positions, or flowcharts. It is about one life*
> *influencing another.*
> – John C. Maxwell (1947), American writer, speaker, and pastor

To further analyse the impact of leadership, Zenger and Folkman conducted research into the effect of leadership on the performance of direct employees. It is made clear here that the effect of good leadership at the top level will result in good leadership at lower levels. Top managers who are perceived as being very effective will therefore work with middle managers who are also rated as being very effective. Similarly, the converse relationship applies: if top managers receive a poor assessment, then their middle managers will also be perceived as being less effective. The reason for this is that leadership is contagious and creates a domino effect. It is therefore interesting to see whether this also has an effect on employee performance. When the effectiveness of middle managers is plotted against employee performance in a graph, it shows that contagion of leadership also applies here. Employees

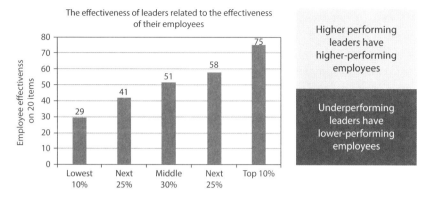

Figure 1.8: Results from research among 2,065 leaders. (Source: Zenger & Folkman, 2012)

who work with a 'good' manager will perform better, and when leadership is rated as 'excellent', employees also show an excellent performance (see Figure 1.8).

The same findings have been observed in an array of cases within various educational organizations by Academica. As described in the case concerning education leaders in the Netherlands, we see that the top of the educational organization (i.e. the Executive Board) determines the impact of school leaders in the layers below and, thereafter, for team leaders and coordinators – when it comes to leadership, the top level sets the bar, leadership effectiveness filters down, and lower organizational levels improve as a result. We see that each level also increases in its effectiveness; where the top scores are higher, the effectiveness of the level below will, on average, also score higher when compared with the scores of other organizations (see Figure 1.7).

If we study this over a longer period of time, then we shall also see – if there is a focus on leadership development – improvement across all levels. Evidence for this can now be presented using various case studies in education (primary, secondary, and intermediate vocational education). Figure 1.7 also provides a good representation of a so-called pre- and post-test, in which the bottom line indicates the first measurement, and the top line indicates the second measurement after a year and a half of development.

Summary: We can learn leadership. Your leadership has an impact on both employees (employee retention, productivity, and engagement) and organizational results (turnover, profit, customer satisfaction, learning outcomes). Evidently, better leaders deliver better results.

The demand for excellent leadership across all organizational levels is increasing. A shortage of skilled labour, accelerated digitization, and changing
global relations mean that we have to re-evaluate our own roles and their
impact on our environment with greater scrutiny than before. Even for
organizations that already have good leaders, leadership development brings
added value. Good leaders can evolve from being good to being excellent,
thereby bringing about all the positive effects for everyone involved. In
Chapter 2 we will discover the mechanisms behind this process.

Confucius | 551 BCE–479 BCE

Niccolò Machiavelli | 1469-1527

Thomas Carlyle | 1795-1881

Frederick Taylor | 1856-1915

Max Weber | 1864-1920

Bertrand Russell | 1872-1970

Simone de Beauvoir | 1908-1986

Abraham Maslow | 1908-1970

Peter Drucker | 1909-2005 ····· *The fundamental task of management is to make people capable of joint performance through common goals, common values, the right structure, and the training and development they need to perform and to respond to change.*

John W. Gardner | 1912-2002

Nelson Mandela | 1918-2013

Thomas Kuhn | 1922-1996

Jim Rohn | 1930-2009 ····· *The enemy of great is good.*

Jack Zenger | 1931

Umberto Eco | 1932-2016 ····· *Greatness is not caused by the absence of weakness.*

Jack Welch | 1935-2020

Richard Petty | 1937

Jesse Jackson | 1941

Stephen Kern | 1943

Daniel Goleman | 1946

Anders Ericsson | 1947-2020

John C. Maxwell | 1947

Peter Senge | 1947

Jaap van Muijen | 1960

Otto Scharmer | 1961

Paul J. Zak | 1962 ····· *Management wordt in de nieuwe organisaties een manier om werkelijk het beste in mensen naar boven te halen, waar vertrouwen wordt gegeven en wordt gewerkt vanuit menselijkheid. Dat zorgt voor werkomgevingen die bezield, doelgericht en productief zijn*

Frederic Laloux | 1969

2. The sweet spot

The only way to do great work is to love what you do.
– Steve Jobs (1955–2011)

The fascinating thing about Steve Jobs is that he has developed what is perhaps the most successful product of the current century while also building an extremely successful organization. Despite these achievements Steve Jobs was by no means a perfect leader; in fact, he was not an easy man to be around and possessed many wayward traits. For example, he washed his feet in the toilet to relax, which, of course, baffled many of his employees. Despite such picadilloes, Steve Jobs did one thing very well: he conveyed his passion to his staff with a hypnotic infectiousness. Employees wanted to work towards Apple's organizational goals because Jobs made them enthusiastic about these goals, and because they could identify with his vision.

You may be competent as a leader and might even achieve all your organizational goals; however, if you are not passionate about what you do you will never rise to great heights. Having passion is essential if a leader wants to increase their impact. Passion is contagious and inspires others, but be aware that a lack of passion is also contagious.

Ask yourself: What are the mechanisms for increasing the effectiveness of a professional and a leader and what does this mean for me? Let us take a closer look at this question in the current chapter.

The CPO model

A sweet spot is where a hit or bump results in maximum response for a given effort. In tennis, baseball or cricket, a given stroke will result in greater momentum when the ball hits the racket (or bat) on the sweet spot. (Source: Wikipedia)

If we translate *sweet spot* into the context of a professional organization, it would be that of a mental state in which you are completely absorbed in your work and know how to organize your work for maximum impact. In such a situation, motivation, strengths, and organizational needs unite, and one experiences feelings such as engagement and energetic focus. Accordingly, activities are undertaken without significant effort, as everything seems

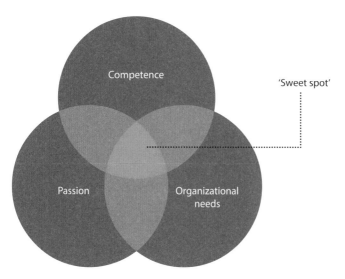

Figure 2.1. The CPO model and the sweet spot.

to go smoothly. We can represent the elements for success using a Venn diagram (see Figure 2.1). The result of this is the CPO model, which clarifies what extremely effective leaders and professionals do; their success does not only come from those competencies at which they excel. Having a passion for your work and expressing the vision of the organization are of equal importance, even though these two elements are not mentioned in a majority of traditional approaches.

If we analyse those moments in which professional reach a high point in their careers, we see that they are able to bring together and focus on the three fundamental elements: competence, passion, and organizational needs (CPO).

1. **Competence**: the combination of knowledge and skills with which you perform well.
2. **Passion**: the things you love doing that energize you (regardless of how good you are at them).
3. **Organizational needs**: knowledge and skills, activities, or services that the organization requires in order to achieve its goal.

Conducting a sweet spot analysis for yourself

To determine your sweet spot, answer the following questions:

– What gives me energy?
– When does it feel like time is not an issue?
– What do other people say are my strengths?

– What have I been successful at in the past?
– What did I subsequently do?
– What feedback do my colleagues give me concerning my added value?
– What is the impact that I both want and can make for my organization and my team?

You can determine your own focus by conducting this analysis of your competence, your passion, and the needs of your organization.

– With competence it is important that you test how your actions are valued by your environment. You may feel that you are good at something, but if others do not experience it that way, you will either have to adjust your image or ensure that others see and appreciate it. Check: Which actions distinguish me from others in my environment and have received a positive evaluation? What do people say when they give me compliments? What is the common thread of success in my career, and what are my actions within this?
– When we talk about passion, we speak about those activities that give energy and satisfaction. Ask yourself the following questions: What activity do I thoroughly enjoy? Which activity makes me feel engaged and energetic? What activity makes me forget about what time it is because I am so completely absorbed in the present?
– The third element, organizational need, concerns the knowledge and skills needed in order to achieve a successful team and/or organization. In the first instance, consider the level at which you can have the greatest impact within your organization; this can concern a team, a project, a department, or even the entire organization. Questions that then become relevant are: What is currently the greatest need of my organization/team? What results that are to be achieved would make the biggest difference to the overall effectiveness of the organization/team? And finally: Which activities would our clients/clients most appreciate?

The overlap of these three areas – the sweet spot – is the area in which you can increase your effectiveness and therefore your job satisfaction, as well as the subsequent positive contagion in regard to your environment.

The CPO model described herein provides support in organizing and planning your prospective career opportunities and performance. You reach your *sweet spot* as described above by finding the overlap between your competence, your passion, and the needs of your organization.

It is not self-evident that this will happen. We often score high on one or two of these elements, but low on the third. There will always be situations in which it is difficult to get all three elements simultaneously. It is for this reason that I would like to point out the possible danger zones in your career. When only two elements in the CPO model overlap, there are three scenarios that are important to recognize and act upon. Staying in one of these three scenarios for too long a time will always cause problems for yourself and your environment.

Three scenarios

What do the three scenarios look like, and what does it mean if I find myself in one of them? Let us discuss all three in greater detail.

1. The first position is when you do possess the necessary competence and undoubtedly know what the organization requires, but the passion for the work concerned is either missing or has disappeared entirely. Accordingly, your work feels meaningless and no longer gives energy. You have the feeling that you are merely 'going through the motions', working routinely, and no longer see the added value of your work. Therefore, we call this the **routine** position. If you have the feeling you are performing routine work for too long and too often, you will use your competence with diminishing consciousness and accuracy. As a result, the competence will no longer remain up-to-date, and will slowly but surely lose its quality. Another possible consequence to this scenario might be that the work demanded requires so much energy from you you end up in a burnout. Every job has routine aspects, this is inevitable. However, the important thing is how you experience your work. If you experience your work increasingly as a monotonous drag, and no longer gain any passion from what you do, you may have to change your work or perhaps even look for alternative job.

2. The second position is when you have passion for what you do and also know what the needs of your organization are, but have not yet acquired the right skills. This can occur when you assume a new role or position: you become a **starter** or novice. The people around you will expect you to perform at some point in time, but if this does not happen quickly enough it can, in their eyes, result in annoyance and/ or lead to criticism. If expectations about this moment are unclear, then problems will arise. These problems will also arise if the super-vision you are provided with is insufficient for you to develop your

competence. When you find yourself in this zone there is a danger that you might lose your passion and eventually drop out. In this position it is important to have clarity concerning the relevant expectations, your induction period, and exactly which qualities/competencies are required of you.

3. The last position is that of the so-called **hobby zone**. In this position, you are passionate about all kinds of activities that give you energy. You are good at these activities, but they provide no real added value for the organization. If you spend too long in this scenario, you run the risk of feeling undervalued and not being noticed. Furthermore, colleagues may avoid you so as not to be bothered by you. Remember it is important that your work remains relevant because, if you stay in the hobby zone for too long, you will eventually become unhappy or the organization will put you on the side-lines. We see that people tend to withdraw into a professional hobby if they receive insufficient feedback about the added value of those activities that are really necessary for the organization. This position may seem nice at first, but in the long run it will prove unsustainable for both the professional and the organization.

An exception to the above can be seen in the deliberate allocation of those people who have a core quality that is not yet required; for example, individuals in technology companies who make certain innovations possible. However, in this case such work is always undertaken according to proper agreements regarding the time and the duration of the use and deployment of such work.

For all three scenarios it must be clear – both to yourself and to your organization – that the missing element is necessary in order to make an effective professional. We need all parts of the CPO model to get into our own *sweet spot*. The unison of all three C-P-O aspects is incredibly powerful and, when this convergence is utilized, your commitment will become a further added value to both yourself and to your organization: **I do what my organization currently needs at a very high level of competence, and this itself gives me energy**. Your challenge is to find the match between what you can do, what you want to do, and what the organization requires. You are responsible for your own career development; those who manage to direct their own development, will experience more control, and thereby reach high points in their career sooner.

It is not only important for managers to explore their own *sweet spot*, but also to analyse and develop those of all their team members. Ultimately, the organization and its leaders will benefit when everyone is in their *sweet spot*; this will then have a positive effect on your entire team and your organization.

Good is not good enough!

The enemy of great is good.
– Jim Rohn (1930–2009), American entrepreneur, author, and motivational
speaker

The main reason why so few organizations and leaders become great is that they stop improving themselves after they have become good. As a result they stop growing, learning, and developing. Previous successes of an organization or leader are often seen as proof that it is good enough for them merely to continue focusing on what is already going well, rather than encouraging them to focus on those areas in which they might excel. We have seen the consequences of this in many organizations over recent decades. Concepts that were previously successful are shown to no longer work, while many big names in business have disappeared in recent years, and will continue to do so in the future (Telfort, Delta Lloyd, NUON, Allsecur, Alex, Volkswagen Beetle). Furthermore, every crisis shows us time and again those leaders and organizations who are flexible and who have enough learning agility to be able to define their role in society in a sustainable manner.

It is important to emphasize that leaders can create and cultivate extra-ordinary performance for their organization by identifying and building on their unique strengths (as well as those of their organization). As we saw in Ericsson's work (Chapter 1), extraordinary achievements are only achieved through *deliberate practice*. You need persistence and passion to do this.

Now let us zoom in on why 'good' is not good enough; a sentiment that is not always received with good humour or applause. Organizations need excellent leaders, and being good is not enough to survive, nor enough to achieve the desired results with your team. You may think that leadership is not the only success factor of an organization and that the disappearance of the brands mentioned above was also caused by the contemporaneous zeitgeist; economic growth or economic contraction in the sector, trends in thinking, culture, COVID-19, and so on. While these influences are undeniable, several studies over the years show that organizations with better leaders have both greater and longer-term success. Indeed, leadership is not the *only* factor influencing the success of an organization. But it is an important factor, and one that we must take very seriously. As Laloux points out, we are now becoming increasingly aware that our traditional thinking about leadership – as well as the way in which we shape and develop it – does not have a sustainable future.

According to traditional thinking and the majority of extant literature, leaders – and the impact of these leaders on their respective organizations – are divided into just two broad categories: they are either 'bad' or 'good'. Continuing from Jim Collins's work, *Good to Great*, Zenger and Folkman's research into the Extraordinary Leader provides even clearer evidence for this argument.[26] Executives can function **poorly**, **well**, or **excellently**. Not two, but three divisions qualify leadership. Perhaps this seems like a small difference at first glance, but it nevertheless has a huge impact when monitoring the effect of the success of both the leader and the organization. Based on Zenger and Folkman's research, there are a number of notable results that underline how you can leverage your potential impact as a leader even more, even in times of success (see box).

Four examples of bad, good, and excellent leadership

1. Good is not the same as excellent

Commercial organizations often depend on their leaders and their sales teams. Figure 2.2 shows a group of 170 executives from one such sales team. The overall leadership effectiveness of sales leaders can be seen on the horizontal axis; this is based on the 360-degree feedback gathered from – among others – the employees of the sales manager, as well as those of his colleagues and his manager. These scores are divided into five levels of effectiveness and are set against the sales of his sales team in millions of euros. Those teams led by the best sales leaders (the top 10 per cent) generate up to six times more sales than those led by the worst-performing sales leaders (lowest scoring 10 per cent).

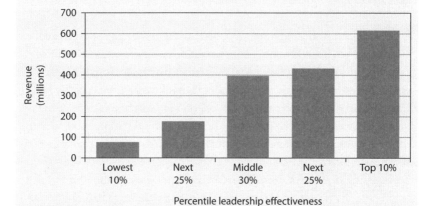

Figure 2.2: 2012 Zenger and Folkman study among 170 sales leaders.

Figure 2.3: Zenger and Folkman study among 30,661 (2012) executives from different sectors.

This graph also shows the significantly lower sales among average-performing leaders (the middle group) when compared with the top leaders. Intuitively, the difference between good and excellent may feel negligible, but when it comes to the impact measured in sales results it can add up to losing out on millions of euros.

As a measurable outcome, sales is – of course – not the only success factor within an organization. This brings me to my second example.

2. Excellent leaders have higher employee engagement and satisfaction

Many organizations see the importance of high employee engagement and satisfaction. This translates into initiatives such as bonuses, flexible working hours, team training, team outings, and improving employee conditions. Such initiatives turn out to be more – or sometimes less – effective in different sectors (just consider the varying effect of bonuses) on increasing employee engagement and satisfaction. Zenger and Folkman's research of more than 30,000 leaders in different industries shows that leadership is the biggest differentiating factor in this regard. In Figure 2.3, the horizontal axis shows the overall leadership effectiveness (obtained from the 360-degree feedback), plotted against employee engagement and satisfaction, both of which are given in percentiles. The top-performing leaders had employees who scored at the 80th percentile for employee engagement and satisfaction, while the worst-performing leaders scored at the 23rd percentile. The difference between the highest and the lowest scoring 10 per cent is enormous, but the difference between top leaders and average good leaders (50–59th percentile) is also noteworthy. Knowing that employee engagement and satisfaction are related to key organizational outcomes, such as customer satisfaction and employee performance, the difference

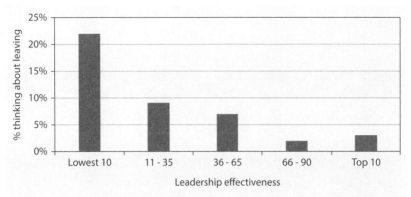

Figure 2.4: Academica 2018 study among 1,150 school leaders.

between average engagement or very high engagement is shown to be an important factor to influence.

3. Excellent leadership connects people

The main reason why employees leave their organization is because the interaction between the leader and their employees is not good. Studies confirming this have been conducted by the Hay Group, YoungCapital, and Gallup, among others. Staff shortages are a problem in many schools, and recruiting and retaining good and qualified teachers is a major challenge for many educational institutions. Research investigating the relationship between leadership effectiveness and the percentage of employees who indicate that they are thinking about leaving has been conducted by Academica within the educational sector (see Figure 2.4); the results of this research are striking. Of the employees who worked for the 10 per cent of executives who performed worst, 22 per cent reported that they intended to leave their current organization. Comparatively, only 3 per cent of employees who worked for the 10 per cent of executives who performed best had thought about quitting. Furthermore, 7 per cent of employees who were working for an average leader (those in the 36–65th percentile), thought about quitting their current educational institution; this percentage is slightly higher for leaders scoring in the top 10 per cent compared with the group directly below. Further research explains that leaders in the top 10 per cent in regard to their effectiveness are able to create a culture of potential mobility and high ambitiousness for their employees, both in a targeted manner and also via consultation with the leader themselves.

Amid the current 'war for talent', a huge waste of time and money results when executives are unable to retain employees and guide them in their professional development. Within this context, the difference between good leaders

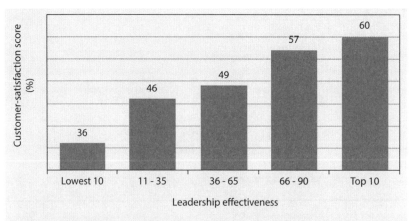

Figure 2.5: Zenger and Folkman's 2012 study at a technical service provider.

and excellent leaders also becomes prominently visible. Excellent leadership connects people and creates a climate in which people want to work and positively reflect, even when they leave the organization.

4. Excellent leadership creates high customer satisfaction

Yet another dynamic can be discovered from the relationship between employee engagement satisfaction and leadership effectiveness in terms of leadership impact: that of customer satisfaction.

The first thing that strikes you when you walk into a store is the way its customers are treated by the store's employees. Are they smiling at you? Or, alternatively, can you hear them talking to one another about things they dislike about their colleagues or their organization? An employee who feels engaged and is satisfied with their work will express these sentiments in a positive way to customers. In all kinds of studies we see that employee engagement and commitment are related to customer satisfaction. Unsurprisingly, a study by Zenger and Folkman, conducted among leaders of a technical service provider, shows that leaders with higher 360-degree feedback scores also have higher customer-satisfaction scores. Furthermore, if we zoom in on the top leaders in this example, we can see whether they make even more of a difference. As is shown in Figure 2.5, this is indeed the case.

In conclusion: highly effective leaders make all the difference between successful and unsuccessful organizations. Consequently, the difference between good and excellent is worth pursuing. Highly effective leaders have a significantly greater impact than merely good leaders, and this thereby influences important organizational outcomes. Excellent leadership can be achieved by each of us. This good news will become increasingly clear to you.

Focus on strengths

Greatness is not caused by the absence of weakness.
– CEO Jack Zenger (1931), Zenger | Folkman

Anyone who has ever undergone a 360-degree feedback or other evaluation process will be aware that we tend to immediately look at the categories with the lowest scores. This human response is the result of years of rigorous conditioning; we measure our performance against the average and tend to strive to improve our weaknesses. Consciously or unconsciously, most of us follow the reasoning that our performance is hampered by below-average skills in one or two aspects. This belief is deeply rooted and is reinforced by numerous experiences throughout the course of our lives. Accordingly, we learn to become more concerned with eliminating perceived weaknesses than we are with building our strengths. However, practice shows that leaders with one or more clear strengths are of far greater value to their organization compared with leaders without such profound strengths. A clear example of this is Steve Jobs, but Facebook's Mark Zuckerberg also shows that he is imperfect. Nevertheless, both have used their strengths to make their companies exemplary.

This evolution in thinking about the impact of strengths mostly started in the 1960s with Peter Drucker, who published various management books.

The fundamental task of management is to make people capable of joint performance through common goals, common values, the right structure, and the training and development they need to perform and to respond to change.
– Peter Drucker (1909–2005), American writer, professor, and consultant in areas such as organizational theory and management.

In 1954 Drucker published his book *The Practice of Management*.[27] In it he describes how leaders can get more out of people. Focusing on objectives and giving employees greater freedom is a philosophy that is very topical today with Laloux's *Reinventing Organizations*.[28]

Figure 2.6: The five habits for working effectively, as introduced by Peter Drucker. (Source: Kumar, 2017)

> *In the new organizations, management is becoming a way to really bring out the best in people, where trust is given and where humanity is the focus. This ensures work environments that are inspired, goal-oriented and productive.*
> – Frédéric Laloux (1969), former associate partner at McKinsey & Company, advisor, and coach

Peter Drucker laid the foundation for modern thinking on leadership and how organizations can achieve better results. He summarizes his focus on achieving a higher effectiveness of managers and leaders in his 'five habits for working effectively'. Peter Drucker was convinced that focusing on one's own strengths, and on the strengths of others, is a very important basis for shaping effective collaboration (see Figure 2.6).

These five habits were later an important source of inspiration for the far more famous 'management guru' Stephen Covey in regard to his work on the seven qualities of effective leadership.[29] Subsequently, Martin Seligman made an important and substantive contribution to thinking and working from strength when he launched the positive-psychology movement and with his work *Learned Optimism*.[30] Some of Seligman's important insights are listed in the box below.

Thinking and working from strength
- Whether you are a pessimist or an optimist depends on how you explain negative events to yourself.

- Pessimists often personalize bad life events, attributing them to permanent and deeper causes.
- Optimists externalize causes of adversity and see them as being fleeting and specific. They attribute positive events to personal, permanent, and ubiquitous causes.
- Optimists are more likely than pessimists to get over a setback and try again.

The consulting firm Gallup, along with its founders Buckingham and Clifton, has also utilized the emergence of thinking about the impact of strengths with the book *Now, Discover Your Strengths*, published in 2001.[31] In their work, Buckingham and Clifton indicate that strength is a combination of talent, skill, and knowledge, and that talent has already crystallized by around 15 years of age. In their eyes, strength is a constant, and is defined as 'a near perfect performance'. They furthermore indicate that talents are innate gifts that cannot be learned.

The work of Zenger and Folkman offers different starting points and insights within the same context, and their research focuses on executives. In their first study using almost 25,000 leaders, Zenger and Folkman presented new insights about the impact of working from strengths. Zenger and Folkman introduced the so-called CPO model (presented earlier in this chapter) to emphasize that strengths alone do not lead to extraordinary performance. Their statement propounds that we, even as adults, remain teachable and developable. In addition, their research shows that we can best use 360-degree feedback not only to identify strengths but also to identify weaknesses. As it turns out, we are the worst predictors of our own strengths and weaknesses.

In their publications, these researchers also describe how strengths can be developed. Indeed, from this research the impact of the further development of strengths becomes clear, as shown at the beginning of this chapter. In addition, Zenger and Folkman showed that you should only focus on a weak competence if it becomes 'fatal' for you within your particular context. Certainly, such a fatal flaw can be addressed and in doing so you will thereby increase your effectiveness. However, these researchers gave professionals new opportunities for development through providing an insight, one that demonstrates that profound strengths lead to far greater impact than merely being 'good'.

The work of Zenger and Folkman, as well as the 2018 Academica study conducted among school leaders, show that leaders with three – and up to a maximum of five – profound strengths can be counted among the top 10 per cent of the most effective leaders in their particular field. From this study,

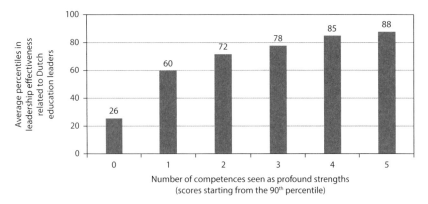

Figure 2.7: The power of profound strengths among Dutch education leaders (Academica research, 2018)

among more than 1,150 education leaders and involving more than 25,000 respondents (employees, colleagues and the leaders or supervisors of these leaders), we see that, rather than being good on average (being without a profound strength), focusing (by developing one profound strength) yields the greatest gains regarding the effectiveness of that leader. See Figure 2.7 for the results of this study.

In the quest for greater effectiveness, the best choice is therefore to focus and expand on those things you do well, that give you energy, and that are also in line with your organization's organizational needs. Zenger and Folkman's research shows that exceptional leaders do a few things very well.[32]

Halo and horn effect

The impact of strengths and fatal flaws on the effectiveness of a professional can be explained by the so-called 'halo and horn effect'.[33]

The **halo effect** is a phenomenon whereby the presence of a certain strength suggests to the observer that other qualities are also present in the individual concerned. If we, as professionals, understand which specific strength it is that suggests the presence of these other qualities, we can target its development towards a specific direction, much like 'spin doctors' do for political leaders. We all remember one of the best-known figures associated with Britain's Labour Party, Alastair Campbell, the pugnacious spin doctor to then Prime Minister Tony Blair.

The opposite of the halo effect is the so-called **horn effect**. The horn effect can be explained as the negative influence on the judgement of an observer

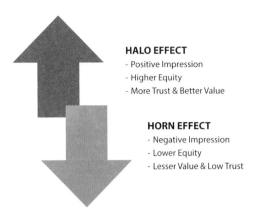

HALO EFFECT
- Positive Impression
- Higher Equity
- More Trust & Better Value

HORN EFFECT
- Negative Impression
- Lower Equity
- Lesser Value & Low Trust

Figure 2.8: The operation of the halo and horn effect.
(Source: MBA Skool Team, 2019)

due to the presence of – to the observer – an unfavourable aspect within the person being observed. The term is derived from the English word 'horn', which, in this context, refers to the horns of the devil. If, through promotion, you secure a different role within the same organization then people will also judge you differently. As an example, while you may never have been asked about your communication skills, this might prove to be an essential skill in your new role as an executive, and one that people around you assess as such. A skill that may have been judged as being barely sufficient in your previous position may now be assessed as being insufficient. This will have a proportionately significant impact on your overall effectiveness and, even if your other qualities are sufficient, the so-called horn effect nevertheless occurs in this situation. Accordingly, you will need to fix this skill in order to have enough impact in your role. It is therefore also important to look at something that is *not* good if such a weakness may become a potential impediment to your professional development.

Summary: We need to get rid of the idea that, for improvement, you always have to work on your weaknesses. Top leaders and professionals make the difference precisely by making use of their strengths. Excellent leadership is therefore a matter of doing a few things very well. A leader will therefore benefit more from developing their strengths rather than focusing on their weaknesses. Furthermore, if you can choose, why would you work on something you do not enjoy anyway? Find your sweet spot!

Now comes the question: 'Is there a formula for success?' Chapter 3 will introduce us to search for this holy grail.

Confucius | 551 BCE–479 BCE

Niccolò Machiavelli | 1469-1527

Thomas Carlyle | 1795-1881

Frederick Taylor | 1856-1915

Max Weber | 1864-1920 — *Charismatic leadership is authority based on the leader's personal qualities and the recognition thereof by their followers.*

Bertrand Russell | 1872-1970

Simone de Beauvoir | 1908-1986

Abraham Maslow | 1908-1970 — *If you only have a hammer, you tend to see every problem as a nail.*

Peter Drucker | 1909-2005

John W. Gardner | 1912-2002

Nelson Mandela | 1918-2013

Thomas Kuhn | 1922-1996

Jim Rohn | 1930-2009

Jack Zenger | 1931 — *Inspirational leadership is not about a single ingredient; it is all about the recipe. It comes about by combining ingredients.*

Umberto Eco | 1932-2016

Jack Welch | 1935-2020

Richard Petty | 1937

Jesse Jackson | 1941

Stephen Kern | 1943 — *Humanity has never strived to slow down.*

Daniel Goleman | 1946

Anders Ericsson | 1947-2020

John C. Maxwell | 1947

Peter Senge | 1947

Jaap van Muijen | 1960 — *Leadership is shaped in the process between the personality of the leader, the characteristics of the followers, and those of the situation.*

Otto Scharmer | 1961

Paul J. Zak | 1962

Frederic Laloux | 1969

3. The quest for the holy grail

There is no secret to success, so don't waste your time looking for such a recipe.
Success is the result of perfectionism, hard work, learning from your mistakes,
loyalty to the people you work for, and persistence.
– Colin Powell (1937), American politician and former general in the United
States Army

Many people still vividly remember the 2016 US presidential election. It was like watching a dramatic and nerve-racking Hollywood movie, starring actors and names known to everyone: Donald Trump and Hillary Clinton. Four years later, in 2020, the same thing seemed to be happening again. Not only was the US holding its breath, but the whole world was following the Presidential race between President Trump and former Vice President Biden. Trump and Biden took contrasting approaches to the presidential race: where Trump values appearing strong – never showing weakness or vulnerability, always presenting himself as being optimistic and positive, and winning at all costs, regardless of the rules – Biden presents a more subdued form of leadership, one characterized by caution, prudence, and thoughtfulness. Accordingly, Biden emphasizes more traditional qualities, such as reliability, integrity, decency, and morality. Despite their different approaches, both strategies have proven to be effective, because both managed to influence their respective followers, something that resulted in a neck-and-neck race.

The following question is often asked in discussions concerning people in leadership positions: is there a single leadership style that is best? The answer is simple: no. Multiple styles can be effective, and their effectiveness depends on many factors – consider the dynamic between the leader and their followers, the ever-changing context in which they operate, and the leader themselves.

Leadership is shaped in the process between the personality of the leader, the
characteristics of the followers, and those of the situation.
– Jaap van Muijen (1960), psychologist

Yet we are always searching for the 'holy grail' of leadership. The amount of information that exists about leadership is staggering; a search for 'leadership' on Amazon.com alone yields more than 60,000 hits. There are many theories and visions about leadership, and the number of articles on this subject are only increasing. Clearly, leadership is very dynamic. That which is effective today may no longer be effective tomorrow.[34] This is not entirely surprising because the concept of leadership itself is – and will continue to be – influenced by societal developments. While some leadership concepts are outdated, others remain current. As an executive within an organization it is therefore very important to be aware of which approach will yield the best results in a certain situation.

Effectiveness of leadership

There is generally still a lack of focus on effective leadership within our current organizational culture. There is also little quantitative research available for pinpointing exactly which leadership behaviours, habits, and competencies yield positive results. Distinctive within this field are large-scale research activities on effective leadership that have been conducted in the last two decades by Zenger and Folkman and the consultancy firm Hay McBer. Mary Fontaine and Ruth Jacobs of Hay and McBer researched different leadership styles, emotional intelligence, and organizational culture based on a sample of 3,871 executives (taken from a database of more than 20,000 executives).[35] Their research describes different leadership styles, each arising from various components of emotional intelligence (see box). When considered individually, these styles appear to have a direct and unique impact on organizational culture. The most striking result of the study, however, is that the most effective leaders use a collection of different leadership styles, each to the right degree, at the right time.

> **Emotional intelligence**
> Emotional intelligence, measured by the **EQ** index, is an addition to the traditional intelligence quotient (IQ). Though the term was first mentioned in 1990 in a scientific article by Mayer and Salovey, it did not immediately enter popular use. This changed in 1995 with the publication of a book of the same name by the American Daniel Goleman. The initial hype that followed the book's publication has since blown over, but the term 'EQ' has remained, despite much criticism from related studies.
>
> Daniel Goleman introduced the concept of emotional intelligence to the general public in 1995 with his bestseller *Emotional Intelligence*. In accordance with the idea introduced above, that leadership styles are environmentally

dependent, Goleman also argues that leaders should also ask themselves which approach best suits the requirements of a given situation. The very best leaders are not restricted to knowing a single style of leadership; they are skilled at several and have the flexibility to switch between these styles according to circumstantial requirements.

Many professionals mistakenly assume that a leadership style is merely a representation of a leader's personal traits, rather than it being a strategic choice. The leadership style you use is a targeted action based on your knowledge, skill, and motivation for achieving organizational objectives.

Research by Zenger and Folkman (using data collected from more than 122,000 leaders from various sectors around the world) indicates that there are a number of – as Zenger and Folkman call them – differentiating competencies; accordingly, competencies can therefore be identified and differentiated from one another. With the vigorous deployment of a single competency, or a combination of two or three competencies, leaders can have an enormously positive effect on employee engagement and, through this effect, customer satisfaction; ultimately this also has a positive effect on their organization as a whole. Zenger and Folkman's research also shows that using the same behaviour is not always the answer, but that finding the right answer is really about a combination of the strength, the focus of the person concerned, their passion, and the needs of their organization at that precise moment. This so-called sweet spot and the possibility to develop from good to excellent has already been discussed in Chapter 2.

> *If you only have a hammer, you tend to see every problem as a nail.*
> – Abraham Maslow (1908–1970), American clinical psychologist

Effective leadership therefore comprises a combination of different 'leadership behaviours': specific ingredients that complement one other. In this way, you can develop your own personal leadership 'recipe' and make optimal use of your own effectiveness. As a professional, the challenge is therefore in recognizing what the organization needs and how you can best fulfil these needs.

Two essential themes are present in the search for the perfect recipe for understanding and applying yourself as a leader: firstly, the ability to **inspire and motivate**; and secondly, the ability to act **quickly and accurately**. I will elaborate on both themes.

Inspiring and motivating: is charisma the secret?

Charismatic leadership is authority based on the leader's personal qualities and
the recognition thereof by their followers.
– Max Weber (1864–1920), German sociologist

When evaluating and analysing particularly influential leaders, the tendency is to focus on the leader's charisma. This tendency is not in itself illogical considering the history of the word *charisma* (which originates from Greek, and which in Christianity means 'a gift from God') and the value that people attach to inspirational capacity. Charisma was believed to be a special gift of the Holy Spirit only bestowed on those individuals chosen by a higher power. Max Weber transferred this word into politics, where it took on a newer meaning: the attraction someone exerts on other people that is experienced as a certain radiance (charismatic leadership) Today, many people still think similarly about leadership, and it is often believed that charisma and inspiring leadership are intended only for those who are 'blessed' or born with this quality.

In recent decades we have seen that leadership theories emphasize the role of leadership in processes of change. Here again we use the presence of charismatic leadership,[36] but also now those of transformational leadership,[37] and inspiring leadership.[38] Leaders are, above all else, inspiring examples for others. Collins's study (Chapter 1) of those organizations capable of changing from *good* to *great* remains an important contribution to thinking about leadership, as well as how leadership impacts organizational outcomes. Despite this, Collins himself was sceptical about the role of leadership in change. However, after analysing his research results Collins eventually stated that 'finally – as should always be the case – the data won'.[39] What Collins had not initially expected was that proper leadership was an important factor in the success of those organizations he had studied. When analysing the behavioural repertoires of these successful leaders, it was revealed that they showed both modesty and willpower.[40] Furthermore, a so-called *executive leader* was present in the successful completion of large-scale change. In Collins' terms, this represents 'level-five' leadership (see box for the elaboration of these five levels).

> **The Five Levels of Leadership: Jim Collins**
> - Level 1: a highly capable individual who makes their contribution through knowledge, talent, and skills.
> - Level 2: a team member who contributes to the achievement of group goals and who works efficiently with other people.

- Level 3: a competent manager who organizes people and resources efficiently so that their set goals are efficiently and effectively achieved.
- Level 4: an effective leader who encourages engagement to, as well as the pursuit of, a clear and compelling vision.
- Level 5: a leader who builds sustainable excellence through a seemingly paradoxical combination of willpower and modesty.

Collins's work is supported by a 7-year longitudinal study, conducted by Hill et al., of 411 school leaders from 160 educational institutions who felt the need to change and improve.[41] Five different types of leader were also distinguished in this same study (see box for the behaviours of the five types of leaders).

The five types of leaders according to Hill et al.

Surgeons – cutting and reorganizing, with a focus on test scores:
- Decisive and astute.
- Understand what is wrong and prioritize according to urgency.
- Apply strict rules and work hard.
- Guide all resources to test scores.

Soldiers – trim and tighten, with an emphasis on the bottom layers of the organization:
- Focused on efficiency and order.
- Run the school as a project manager.
- Tenacious and task-oriented.
- Only focus on internal affairs.

Accountants – invest and grow, with a focus on the top of the organization:
- Resourceful and systematic.
- Provide greater money flow to become stronger.
- Creative accountants.
- Let teachers find out for themselves how they should spend money.

Philosophers – debate and discuss, are focused on values:
- Love to teach and talk about innovation.
- See themselves more as experienced teachers.
- Linguistically and verbally strong.
- Focus on the long term.

Architects – redesign and transform, with an emphasis on long-term impact:
- Want social impact.
- Smart, modest and have vision.
- Take time for school improvement.
- Focus on the environment and community.

So-called *architect leaders*, those school leaders able to achieve sustainable results (i.e. results concerning student examinations and school finances), were found to be the most successful. The characteristics of these leaders are very similar to Jim Collins' level-five leaders. The architect-leader invests in their community, provides a good learning environment, focuses on impact and opportunities, and has a holistic view of public values. Researchers have characterized, among other things, that being clever, modest, and being a visionary are those qualifications possessed by architect-leaders.

'Silver bullet'

Zenger and Folkman investigated the most distinctive leadership competencies possessed by highly successful leaders.[42] Of the 19 leadership competencies (in regard to distinguishing between the top 10 per cent and the bottom 10 per cent of leaders) the 'inspire and motivate others' competency turned out to be the greatest lever for generating employee engagement. Where we previously saw that employee engagement generates a very important dynamic for achieving better organizational results, we now see that this competency distinguishes top leaders from average effective leaders. For this reason, the 'inspire and motivate others' competency is referred to by these researchers as the *silver bullet*.

While the ability to inspire and motivate others does indeed act as a catalyst for increasing leadership effectiveness, it is not all-determining. Leaders who employ multiple powerful competencies will achieve the greatest results. I will discuss this in greater detail in the section concerning the various core ingredients of inspirational leadership. An interesting phenomenon is that this competency is assessed by employees as being the most desirable behaviour for their leaders to possess. When surveyed, employees of the leaders who took part in the study were asked the following question: 'What behaviour would you like to see in your manager?', all employees who answered the question put the 'inspiring and motivating others' competency in the top three most desired competencies. Evidently, employees want inspiring leaders.

You can learn to inspire

Zenger and Folkman are committed to debunking myths about innate leadership and showing that leadership development works.[43] Like Collins, they indicate that data must be the guiding principle when making statements about leadership and its developability through learning. The question as to whether you can learn inspirational leadership was therefore an important research question, one that was viewed Zenger and Folkman from a data-based perspective. Accordingly, they followed a group of more than 300 leaders over a 18–24 month period. During this period, the leaders received a concrete action plan and specific feedback for increasing their 'inspiring and motivating others' competency. Results were clear in the post-test: leaders moved from the 42nd percentile to the 70th percentile regarding their ability to inspire and motivate others – something that Zenger and Folkman called significant progress.

Contrary to popular belief, inspirational leadership is not something to be displayed occasionally, for instance 'at my annual soapbox speech in my organization's auditorium'. Inspiring and motivating others is something that leaders should commit to and exercise every day. Being inspiring means that everything you do as a leader on a daily basis has an impact on how the people around you perceive and experience you; being inspiring and motivating is a catalyst for leadership effectiveness. Through inspiring leadership you can bright about the positive 'contagion' of the environment to the greatest degree possible. Employees who feel emotionally involved and engaged will be more enthusiastic and more committed to realizing organizational goals; furthermore, as a leader, you will also prefer to see such enthusiasm among your employees on a daily basis. In his research into new organizational structures, Laloux shows that, in what he refers to as teal-coloured organizations, the presence of leadership can create a continuously inspiring work environment (see the next chapter and Chapter 1, Figure 1.3).[44] Given the different transitional phases through which organizations and the people who work in them go, different needs and opportunities exist when it comes to inspiring and motivating. Accordingly, there is no standard formula that works for everyone and for every situation.

The core ingredients for inspirational leadership

Inspirational leadership is not about a single ingredient; it is all about the recipe. It comes about by combining ingredients.
– Jack Zenger (1931), CEO Zenger | Folkman, author of several books on organization and leadership development

Now that we know the importance of being able to inspire and motivate others as leaders, the following question remains: 'How can you be more inspiring as a leader?' Zenger and Folkman's research also provides interesting insights for answering this query.[45] Using their database, Zenger and Folkman undertook a closer examination of more than 1,000 inspiring leaders in order to identify those specific behaviours that ensured the leader's received high scores for 'inspiring and motivating others' from other individuals within their environment (colleagues, employees, and other professionals). Their conclusion was not unequivocal: every leader can be inspiring in a different way.

Six inspiring leadership styles (see box below) were then identified based on this research, and it was found that inspirational leaders usually used one or two of these six leadership styles. The different styles use different ingredients, but it is interesting to note that all the leaders examined used the following two essential behaviours:

– **They are able to make an emotional connection with their employees.**
– **They communicate powerfully and prolifically.**

Each style has a different emphasis, and some examples of how to connect with others according to these different styles of inspiration are shown below.

– Starting every meeting by sharing a positive experience; making sure you radiate positive energy.
– Interpreting the vision of the future according to different stories that are both easy to understand and inspiring, while also showing your own passion for this vision.
– Actively questioning people about their ideas as to how things could be done differently, positively reflecting on this, and indicating that you have confidence in your team.
– Making personal contact with your people that is not solely based on their expertise. Collect facts and present them with confidence.
– Identifying common values; share information and try to be as transparent as possible.
– Greet everyone in every meeting and make eye contact with each of them. Recognize when people have put in extra effort.

Six inspiring leadership styles

Motivator: *I share my enthusiasm for the assignment and trust its positive contagion.*
These leaders show passion, vitality, strength, and power. They are dynamic rather than passive, more outgoing than introverted, and good at creating energy. With these skills they encourage their team to take action, while also managing maintain high levels of enthusiasm during projects. This keeps employees enthusiastic, even when presented with impossible tasks. They also remain optimistic and have the strength to overcome disillusionment and disappointment. Difficult goals are achievable for these leaders because they continue to believe they can reach them.

Visionary: *I develop new strategies for and with the team so we can achieve our goals.*
These leaders create a clear, concrete, and vivid picture of the future. They think ahead and think strategically, instead of just tactically and concretely. In doing this they make ambitious and challenging goals seem achievable. This leadership style ensures that teams and employees accept a new direction, keep the end goal in mind, and do not get lost in detail. Their employees have a good understanding of how their ow work contributes to larger organizational goals and see this contribution as being valuable. Through their vision, these leaders are able to achieve consensus and agreement concerning the means by which these organizational goals are to be reached.

Developer: *I encourage greater collaboration and trust between team members.*
These leaders are strongly focused on creating positive relationships and have a keen interest in other people's ideas and opinions. They treat others with respect and dignity, remain positive, and try to get the best out of their team. They achieve organizational goals because they 'pull' their team, providing their team with the right insights and encourage it to work towards organizational goals. While most leaders *push* their employees to achieve goals, effective leaders know how to *pull* employees. Employees feel valued and respected; this leadership style reduces conflict while simultaneously stimulating healthy competition. The team experiences a sense of unity.

Expert: *I make my knowledge and expertise available and do so to support my team with a plan.*

These leaders provide valuable up-to-date information to the team and can find innovative solutions to tough problems. They increase their team's technical understanding and use personal expertise to help implement solutions. This style ensures that teams and employees build their expertise to successfully complete technological challenges, they are successful in finding the best and fastest solution and achieve organizational goals faster because they are able to solve complex problems more easily.

Principled: *I remind my people that others outside of our team should be able to count on us.*

These leaders emphasize and demonstrate a high degree of integrity; they encourage others to follow rules and establish procedures. They practice what they preach and thereby act as role models. This leader does not expect others to compromise on what is right or ethical. This leader ensures that employees find satisfaction in pursuing a worthwhile goal, one that is greater than themselves. Employees experience a strong basis of trust, they recognize the usefulness of rules and procedures, and perform tasks consistency and precision.

Driver: *I encourage a faster pace and focus the team on meeting the deadline.*

These leaders place an emphasis on achieving the goals of their organization. The leader meets deadlines and commitments regardless of what this might demand. They believe that being on time and within budget are necessary results, not great aspirations. Employees get energy by achieving measurable and concrete goals; they are therefore more likely to overcome challenges that require a lot of effort and energy because they respond quickly and decisively. Employees are motivated to perform 'difficult' or 'tedious' work and also adhere to set deadlines and budgets.

By mastering different leadership styles and consciously deploying these styles according to situational demands you will increase the likelihood of being effective. If deployed too one-sidedly, however, every leadership style can also result in negative as well as positive effects. For example, if you focus too strongly on the driver style, you may achieve the formulated objectives, but there is also a risk that those within your environment will assess your intentions as being less sincere. In addition, an overly strong and one-sided commitment to the developer style will afford you high appreciation regarding integrity and honesty as a leader on the one hand, but on the other hand there is a chance that you will have a lower impact when it comes to achieving the objectives of your organization. It is precisely through the combination of several leadership styles and competencies that the downside of a particular leadership style can be mitigated or compensated; this will increase your leadership effectiveness and make the most of your leadership strength. It is important that you consciously choose your personal leadership 'recipe' in order to use a personal success formula that best suits your organization throughout its transition. Be aware of the effect of your choices and make sure that you supplement and adjust where necessary.

In conclusion, leaders can be inspiring and motivating in different ways. Leaders who use a combination of the different styles experience greater benefit than leaders who use only one style.

High performing: focus on speed and quality

Humanity has never strived to slow down.
– Stephen Kern (1943), author, and recipient of the Guggenheim Fellowship Prize
in the Humanities category

In our current era everything is moving with increasing speed. We are also becoming increasingly aware of our continuous striving to be *even faster*; accordingly, the following question arises with increasing pertinence and regularity: But what about the quality of our actions? 'Slow' movement (such as the preparation of slow food) is not a counter-movement to this fast-paced trend, but rather responds with: 'Be fast when it is wise to be fast and slow when slowness is required'. In education, we see this theme reflected in, among other things, the book *Bordwerk en aantekeningen* ('Chalkboard writing and notes') by Marcel Schmeier.[46]

The question you should ask yourself is: 'Is my focus on quality or speed?' Most people focus on either quality or speed. After all, it is difficult to guarantee quality when tasks have to be completed at a rapid pace, or so it is often thought. People prefer to work more slowly in order to guarantee the quality of the process concerned and to minimize the chance of error. For those who want to become highly effective leaders, however, it is important to master both.

High performing leaders show both speed and quality when achieving successful results. When quality remains high, speed is one of the most important factors whereby organizations can achieve better results and returns. Why? Well, because speed of action and making choices has become increasingly important within our current organizational culture. This is not only true for commercially driven organizations, wherein we have always seen how reacting quickly to market developments is an important quality. With the advent of COVID-19 pandemic, the need for civil society to be agile and fast becomes increasingly clear. 'High performing schools' – schools that have a clear and shared vision of learning, and which continuously work through learning teams to improve the education they provide – switched from face-to-face classroom teaching to online lessons and remote learning within a week. These schools were able to organize this change while simultaneously maintaining good-quality education. This could only be realized – as we see in the work of E.D. Hirsch[47] – because of the substantial, solid core of general knowledge they share which gives these High performing schools the flexibility to learn new things fast.

In a sense, the growing need to be able to combine both speed and quality reflects what is happening in society: speed has increased in every aspect of life and in every sector. To ensure their ongoing existence, organizations must significantly increase the speed at which they operate and make important decisions. Every sector needs a sustainable business model in which the demand for rapid response increases while the demand for quality remains. We therefore see three trends in so-called high performing organizations:[48]

1. They quickly identify problems and trends.
2. They respond quickly to problems and trends.
3. They quickly organize necessary changes.

As André de Waal described in his analysis of more than 230 national and international studies and 2,600 surveys – *Hoe bouw je een High Performance Organisatie?* ('How to Build a High Performance Organization') – there are five success factors that characterize high performing organizations:

Five success factors for a high-performing organization
1. The **management** is of a **high quality** and combines integrity and coaching leadership with **fast decision-making**.
2. The **culture** of a high-performing organization involves everyone intensively through an open culture and dialogue aimed towards **actions for realizing better performance**.
3. There is a **long-term orientation** towards customers, suppliers, and fellow cooperating organizations, but also towards management and its employees. **New leaders are recruited and developed from within the organization**.

4. A high-performing organization has a unique distinction in the market and allows **all employees to continuously contribute to the improvement and renewal** of its processes, services, and products.
5. The employees are diverse in terms of background and expertise and complement one other well through good cooperation. They are **flexible and resilient** and mainly work to achieve the result or objective.

Jack Welch already wrote the mantra of **speed – simplicity – self-confidence** for General Electric back in 2000. Twenty years later we see that we not only find speed to be very important, but also that there is a relationship between leadership speed and leadership effectiveness. The interpretation of the term 'leadership speed' does not suggest a one-sided focus on doing something quickly; it also keeps quality in mind, based on a common goal. The definition provided by Zenger and Folkman as a result of their research into this subject is a simple formulation, one that is now widely used:

Speed of leadership = the ability to do things in a good way quickly

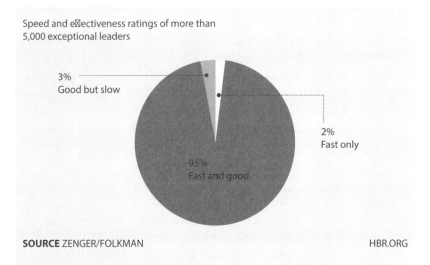

Speed and effectiveness ratings of more than 5,000 exceptional leaders

3%
Good but slow

2%
Fast only

95%
Fast and good

SOURCE ZENGER/FOLKMAN   HBR.ORG

Figure 3.1: Effective leaders must be good and fast. (Source: Zenger & Folkman, 2015b)

Leadership speed

The results of Zenger and Folkman's survey of 50,000 leaders showed that we need both competencies to be seen as exceptional leaders.[49]

Of all leaders, 5,711 belonged to the top 10 per cent of executives (they scored at the 90th percentile or higher of leadership effectiveness), 2 per cent of which (114 leaders) were rated as being fast, but not extremely effective; 3 per cent (170 leaders) were rated as effective, but not fast; while 95 per cent (over 5,400 leaders) were rated as being very effective and fast. Very effective leaders know how to combine both speed and efficiency (see Figure 3.1).

But how do I increase my leadership speed? We see that Zenger and Folkman offer seven tools for doing this as informed by their research (see box).[50] Depending on your own situation and challenges, you can focus on one or more factors.

Seven factors that increase leadership speed

1. Clarify vision and strategy

You can continuously clarify vision and strategy for the organization. This is important because it allows employees to fulfil their role within the organization with greater speed and efficacy. If everyone is on the same page, it is easier to achieve objectives within the organization faster. In the absence of a clear strategy, the pace will slow down and problems concerning quality will increase. Sometimes leaders have a clear strategic direction, but fail to share their vision with others. An example of how things should be done is Tjeerd Jegen, CEO of HEMA (a renowned Dutch high street retailer) since 2015, who shared his vision and strategy of how to maintain HEMA as an organization. As a result, employees became engaged and more creative in thinking about solutions.

2. Setting stretch goals and a high standard

When employees are given easy goals to achieve, they are more likely to work in a relaxed and slow manner. However, setting stretch goals coupled with a high standard reinforces the need for employees to focus on improving their speed. These goals encourage people to focus and keep going. Leaders who set goals increase the pace. An example of a one-sided focus on a stretch goal, without a high standard, can be seen in the Samsung Galaxy Note 7. Samsung needed to urgently beat Apple, and in 2016 they hastily introduced a new smartphone to the market. Its production was discontinued that same year due to several problems.

3. Communicate powerfully

When everyone understands where the organization wants to go and what the objectives are, employees will work faster and at the same time guarantee quality. If employees do not receive the correct information, uncertainty arises and the risk of errors increases. As a result, organizational objectives are achieved less quickly. Communication is the easiest skill to learn; yet people often do not communicate well, which leads less speed and more errors. We see that in a time of crisis we want to be informed about what we can and cannot do, as well as the reasoning behind this ability. The almost-weekly press conferences held during the COVID-19 crisis are a good example of powerful communication, though whether this communication was clear enough remains uncertain.

4. Consider external perspectives

As a leader, you do not only have to think within the framework of your own company, you can also look outside it in order to spot trends and changes at an early stage. We are often too busy with internal affairs and problems, causing us to lose sight of customer issues, competitors, or changes in our world. It is also a good idea to position people that have an external focus within your own organization. If, for example, in education I am a specialist in the field of language, it is important to look from within my own field of expertise at how society values language, but also to look at what the future requirements of that society will be for language itself. What does this mean for our vision of the profession and for my school's curriculum? These are important questions to ask.

5. Inspiring and motivating others

Employees feel that they are an essential part of the success of the organization. As mentioned before, most leaders push their employees to achieve goals, but inspirational leaders also know how to *pull* employees to increase speed and quality. Taking people into a future that is yet to be clearly defined, but that we can nevertheless form a picture about together in regard to how it might look, is the best way to inspire people. Barack Obama is still seen as a man who *pulled* people along with his motto 'Yes We Can'.

6. Innovate

Leaders with a focus on innovation are always looking for a fresher, more efficient, and faster way of working. Increasing speed and quality using standard procedures is impossible; this requires innovative and creative input. There is always a better way. The online delivery industry is a good example of this. The way in which this sector has manifested itself, with a continuous introduction of new ways of acting quickly and with high quality, is remarkable. Hybrid solutions (whereby workers can work from home as well as in the office) are both a newly introduced and newly accepted means of working according to different situations and possibilities.

7. Organizational change

These leaders focus on and are committed to *agility*. Agile organizations are mobile, agile, and able to act quickly and decisively. The willingness to take risks makes people act faster. The transformation to agile organizations was introduced earlier in this book as a paradigm shift for the thinking and acting of organizations. Switching from printing banners for large conventions and congresses to making splash screens and masks for companies during the COVID-19 crisis provides a wonderful example of the agility of organizations: responding quickly to failing demand and responding to new demand.

We see that these seven factors and the five pillars of De Waal's research overlap considerably.

Summary: Is there a success formula for leadership? Every situation requires a different emphasis. However, the human factor is becoming increasingly important. We see that the challenge is to involve all people in the organization (i.e. inspire them) from a common vision to a shared goal. This makes it possible to act agile, fast, and better in order to achieve goals.

In the next chapter we will investigate how we can increase the engagement of people to achieve success together in our organization. The concept of trust will play a central role in this.

Confucius | 551 BCE–479 BCE

Niccolò Machiavelli | 1469-1527

Thomas Carlyle | 1795-1881

Frederick Taylor | 1856-1915

Max Weber | 1864-1920

Bertrand Russell | 1872-1970

Simone de Beauvoir | 1908-1986

Abraham Maslow | 1908-1970

Peter Drucker | 1909-2005

John W. Gardner | 1912-2002

Nelson Mandela | 1918-2013

Thomas Kuhn | 1922-1996

Jim Rohn | 1930-2009

Jack Zenger | 1931

Umberto Eco | 1932-2016

Jack Welch | 1935-2020

Richard Petty | 1937

Jesse Jackson | 1941

Stephen Kern | 1943

Daniel Goleman | 1946 ○----● *People need to be smarter with their emotions*

Anders Ericsson | 1947-2020

John C. Maxwell | 1947

Peter Senge | 1947

Jaap van Muijen | 1960

Otto Scharmer | 1961

Paul J. Zak | 1962 ○----● *Trust is kind of this economic lubricant. When trust is high, morale is high…*
Higher trust environments produce individuals who are happier.

Frederic Laloux | 1969

4. Impact on the team

People need to be smarter with their emotions.
– Daniel Goleman (1946), author, and science journalist for the *New York Times*

In 2018, a primary school in the Netherlands was assessed as being 'very weak' by the Education Inspectorate. Despite hearing in advance that the school was not performing very well, the school's newly appointed principal was nevertheless surprised by this very severe judgment. She called the team together and said: 'From now on we can only do better; and indeed we will do better.' She then set out a plan of action and expressed confidence in the team – 'I look forward to working with you on this task, which will involve us working hard and working together intensely. We are going to create a high-performing school together.' The positive sound in her voice, her positive appearance, and her positive and clear powerful intention were picked energetically by the team of teachers and internal mentors. Two years after this event and the school is already on its way to becoming an excellent school. The school team is extremely engaged, it works according to a shared vision of learning in order to provide excellent education for all its students. This is the result of doing the right things together within a professional learning community.

Relationship and results

A study by Bas Koene (director and researcher, Rotterdam School of Management), *Organizational culture, leadership, and performance in context: trust and rationality in organizations*, conducted in 50 branches of a large supermarket chain, looked at the effect of the branch manager's leadership. It also focussed on the culture of these particular supermarkets in regard to their operating results.[51] From this research it was found that the leadership of the branch managers mainly influenced aspects of internal social relationships, such as motivation and trust. By contrast, the structure of the organization was found to mainly have an impact on the clarity and comprehensibility of the organization's goals, tasks, and roles.

When we ask people about those qualities that they think make great leaders so successful, they often refer to the ability to use the right strategy, the possession of a clear vision, and the ability to achieve results. However, leadership initially starts with something much more basic: emotion management. The reason why the actions of a leader are so important lies in the way our human brains function. People are susceptible to the emotions of others, which is explained by scientists as emerging from the 'open loop' of the limbic system, known as the emotional centre of the brain (see the box below for an example). A 'closed loop', such as the cardiovascular system, is self-regulating. Comparably, an open loop depends on external sources for the ability to adjust itself. This means that we depend on our emotional connection with others for our own emotional stability. The open loop system is one of interpersonal regulation. This means that signals that other people send us can cause changes in our own cardiovascular functioning, our sleep rhythm, and even our immune system. In short, our physiological systems respond to each other.[52]

Action–reaction

In the intensive care unit it is very important that people have the support of someone they trust; such a comforting presence causes a patient's blood pressure to drop and the accumulation of fatty acids in the veins to slow down.[53]

It is quite recognizable that our physiological systems respond to one another. Just think of couples in love and the warm feeling that arises in people when they see someone with whom they are in love. This feeling is created because we have an interpersonal relationship with the other person, as a result of which our brains release oxytocin – also known as the 'hug hormone'. Our physiological systems are also activated in social situations; we automatically adapt our behaviour according to other people within our environment. Research has shown that, after having a positive conversation with one another, people show congruence in their physiological values; this means, for example, that they have the same heart rate, something that was not the case before they had the conversation.

We see the same effects in the office during meetings. Team members inevitably adopt feelings from each other and from the leader. For example, Caroline Bartel, and Richard Saavedra studied 70 groups of people who worked together in various sectors (ranging from groups of nurses to groups of accountants), and discovered that at the end of a 2-hour meeting they all shared the same moods – whether good or bad – independently of quarrels between colleagues.[54] A study by Yale University School of Management also found that moods affect work effectiveness; a cheerful mood appears to have a positive effect on collaboration, openness, and business results.

People derive their emotions from others, therefore the individual who is most looked at when it comes to emotions in the workplace will be an employee's superior or leader. The leader thus plays the most important role when it comes to emotional contagion, because they are the one who act as role models. This goes to show that the role of the leader is critical when creating an engaged team. Highly effective leaders are aware of this.

Several months ago a client asked me the following question: 'Is it possible to focus both on delivering results and building positive relationships with your team? How do the leaders who are able to do this bring this about?'

Many people argue that, if either of these things is done well, it is nearly impossible to do the other equally well. The 360-degree feedback data from Zenger and Folkman shows that the best leaders (those who scored in the 90th percentile of effective leadership) do manage to be both good at creating an engaged team and at delivering results.[55] What specific behaviours do these leaders exhibit that are both results-oriented and people-oriented? To investigate the specific characteristics and behaviour of these leaders, we looked at the group of leaders who scored high in both of these aspects.

A remarkable discovery was made: young leaders especially excel in their ability to create a working atmosphere in which employees are both highly effective and simultaneously enjoy themselves in the workplace. More specifically, leaders under the age of 30 are two to three times more likely to be effective at this than their older colleagues. This effect is reflected when looking at the positions that these leaders hold, because the age of a leader often correlates with their position: supervisors were better than their senior managers in generating engagement and achieving results.

We see that younger leaders use their social skills more in order to achieve the necessary results. Older and more experienced leaders would also clearly benefit if they would do this. We also see that more women than men are able to connect both of these aspects. Finally, when under pressure, we see that we tend to focus more on outcomes than on relationships. Chapters 7 and 8 return to the subject of differences in generations and the differences between the displayed and perceived leadership of men and women.

Six behavioural bridges

How come there are leaders who know how to find a good balance between focusing on results and stimulating employee engagement? According to their research, Zenger and Folkman identified six of what they call 'behavioural bridges' for connecting these two elements. These functions are powerful combinations that can accelerate leadership effectiveness by creating an engaged team:

1. Communicate clear strategy and direction.
2. Inspire and motivate.
3. Achieving stretch goals.
4. Integrity and trust.
5. Supporting others in their development.
6. Learning agility.

These behaviours can be viewed from a focus on achieving results as well as from a focus on the creation of a good relationship (i.e. being people-oriented). In the box below, the six behavioural bridges are explained from the two elements they serve.

The six behavioural bridges for combining results and people orientation

Communicate clear strategy and direction
Results-oriented
We achieve top results when we have clarity about our direction and understand the strategy by which we can achieving it.
People-oriented
When people do not understand a particular vision, they become dissatisfied because they do not know which direction to take. Leaders who can effectively and clearly communicate this vision and direction ultimately have more engaged teams.

Inspire and motivate
Results-oriented
Results can be achieved in different ways; a commonly used method is by working hard as a manager and 'pushing' people in the right direction. However, we have to guide people and take them along with us. If we inspire and motivate people so that our employees not only work for results because they have to, but also because people like to dedicate themselves to achieving these results, then we *pull*. The right dynamics of *push* and *pull* provide us with the best results.
People-oriented
Inspirational behaviour unleashes a certain energy in employees so that they can fulfil organizational goals for optimal achievement. Accordingly, employees feel that they are making a positive difference through their work. Leaders who

can generate loyalty, dedication, passion, and enthusiasm in their team, and that also inspire their people, excel at creating a positive work environment.

Achieving stretch goals
Results-oriented
Setting stretch goals that are accepted by team members has the power to push people to get more out of themselves. In this way the bar is set high for everyone.
People-oriented
When people are involved in the decision-making process and are allowed to co-decide, or contribute to decisions on, stretch goals they will feel valued and competent.

Possesses a high degree of integrity and inspires confidence
Results-oriented
A leader who wants to encourage their employees to achieve intended results must first of all gain their confidence. In this instance, trust and employee motivation go hand in hand. When employees trust their leader, they are more likely to see their intentions as fair. In addition, they feel less likely to be manipulated or abused.
People-oriented
The leader serves as a role model, employees derive their emotions and behaviour from him or her. The leader sticks to their word, and puts it into action to pursue their own objectives; they also invest in the relationship with their employees. The result of this is that employees trust that their leader treats people with integrity, which makes them want to work harder to achieve set goals.

Develops others
Results-oriented
Leaders who focus on developing their people reap the benefits of this process in the results they manage to achieve. People who develop continuously are more productive.
People-oriented
The leader is committed to employees development. Most people have the desire to develop themselves and would like to have the opportunity to learn new skills and competencies. Ultimately, this increases performance, but it simultaneously creates a pleasant organizational culture that is both stimulating and engaging. This culture retains valuable employees, but also attracts new and potential employees.

Learning agility

Results-oriented

The leader is open to feedback and knows how to implement this feedback in the right way in order to optimize results. Employees will alert the executive when they make a mistake and, because the supervisor is open to this, effectiveness at work increases.

People-oriented

Leaders who ask for feedback from others, and who are committed to improving the organization are both highly respected and valued. Their coachability stands as an example for everyone.

In conclusion, combining a focus on results with a genuine interest in people is an important skill because it is such a powerful combination. This combination has an impressive impact on effectiveness and engagement in regard to both leaders and employees.

A positive work culture

> *The Netherlands Centre for Occupational Diseases (NCvB) has noted an increase in the number of people who report to their company doctor with a burnout. Cause: the combination of an excessive workload and lack of peer support (see Figure 4.1).*[56]

Burnout is the number one occupational disease worldwide, and its consequences are huge. The increased workload, mutual competition, continuous change, and the urge to innovate cause employees to experience considerable stress. Organizational psychologists show that an overly stressful work environment is not only harmful to the productivity and health of employees, but also to organizational results, the amount of cost incurred due to occupational diseases, as well as the to the overall effectiveness of the organization. A large-scale survey of more than 3,000 employees, conducted by Swedish psychologist Anna Nyberg, has shown that there is a relationship between leadership behaviour and employee heart disease.[57]

At the beginning of this chapter it was described how our physiological systems respond to each other; as a leader, you therefore contribute to the well-being of your employees. The components of a burnout mirror those of engagement. If we assume this, employees who experience burnout therefore become unengaged or less engaged. Many organizations have already tried to reduce this occupational disease through measures such as introducing

Percentage of employees aged 15-65 with burnout complaints.

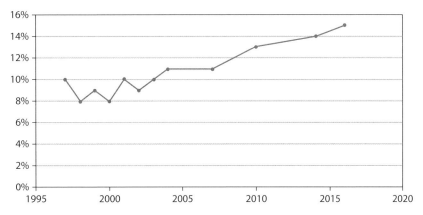

Figure 4.1: The percentage of employees with burnout complaints has increased in recent years. (Source: CBS, 2017)

office fitness rooms and increasing working from home. However, scientific research shows that the emotional well-being of employees mainly depends on their engagement to the company. More than anything else, employee engagement predicts employee well-being, and indeed employees themselves prefer well-being in the workplace over material benefits.

The leader is crucial when it comes to employees experiencing things positivity. Sy et al. have investigated leaders' moods and the emotional contagion of these moods.[58] First, the results of this investigation show that leaders who have a positive mood influence their employees in a positive way: employees are therefore more likely to experience a positive mood than a negative one. Second, teams led by a positive leader are more coordinated and require less effort to complete tasks.

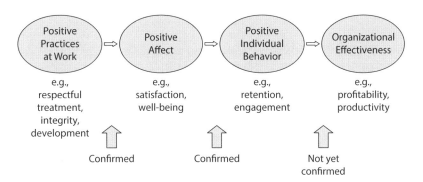

Figure 4.2: The four principles that create a positive work culture. (Source: Cameron et al., 2011)

As a leader there are several ways through which you can create a positive culture in which employees feel engaged and in which their emotional well-being is guaranteed. Researchers Cameron et al. identity four principles that can help leaders create a positive work culture (see Figure 4.2).[59]

Four principles that create a positive work culture

Work on social relationships
A large number of empirical studies confirm that positive social connections at work produce highly desirable results. Sarah Pressman of the University of California showed that the odds of premature death are 20 per cent higher for obese people, 30 per cent higher for excessive drinkers, and 50 per cent higher for smokers. But one cause is head and shoulders above the rest: having bad social relationships, which increases the risk of premature death by as much as 70 per cent.

Show empathy
As a leader, you have a huge impact on how employees feel. Brain studies show that when employees evoke a particular image of their unfriendly or non-empathetic boss, activity in those areas of the brain that are associated with avoidance and negative emotions increased. In contrast, leaders who show empathy evoke resilience in their employees during challenging periods, such as at times when employees experience increased workloads.

Make an effort to help
If you have ever had a manager who went to great lengths to help you when they did not have to do so, then the chances are that, as a result, you became very loyal to this manager. Jonathan Haidt of New York University's Stern School of Business shows in his research that when leaders are not just honest, but also self-sacrificing, their employees are moved and inspired to become more loyal and committed.[60]

Encourage people to talk to you, especially about their problems
Psychological safety is extremely important to employees. Research by Harvard's Amy Edmondson shows that a psychologically safe work environment – an environment in which leaders are inclusive (see Chapter 9), are humble, and encourage employees to be open – leads to better performance and results.[61]

Creating a positive work culture is an important part of the success of an organization. Such a culture promotes well-being and engagement among employees and will thereby bear fruit for organizational results.

New meaning to work and the organization

In the quest to give new meaning to employees' work, and thereby create a high level of engagement, it is now time to take a closer look at the work of Laloux (also briefly discussed above).[62] In his book *Reinventing Organizations* Laloux describes a new organizational model for what he calls 'evolutionary teal' organizations (a term born from the analysis of multiple organizational types as expressed in the colours red, amber, orange, green, and teal). Accordingly, employees do not merely show their rational and professional side, as they can also give their emotional, intuitive, and spiritual sides consideration and importance. The starting point of this system is to consider the organization as a living organism, for which Laloux uses the term *teal-coloured organizations*. These organizations have three common characteristics: self-management, wholeness, and evolutionary purpose. These characteristics reinforce one another (see box).

Laloux's three characteristics of teal-coloured organizations

Self-management
Work effectively, even on a large scale, with a system based on equal relationships, without the need for hierarchy or overall consensus.

Wholeness
Applications that invite us to restore our inner wholeness, and also to bring this about in everyone else working, instead of holding a narrow 'professional' identity.

Evolutionary purpose
Organizations are seen as alive and as having their own sense of direction. Rather than trying to predict and control the future, members of the organization are invited to listen and understand what the organization wants to become and what goals it has in order to actively participate within it.

According to Laloux, we are able to create more inspired and meaningful organizations together, or else we are able to transform existing organizations into being inspired and meaningful. We must get away from ego trippers and on the way towards a new impetus whereby people can make a difference together. This requires a different form of leadership for everyone; Laloux proposes shared leadership for creating more inspired and meaningful organizations, a shared leadership with inner justice and purpose as the primary motivator. Self-management in teal-coloured organizations have eight basic principles that will be recognizable recognize from those studies described earlier. I will briefly mention and elaborate on these principles in the box below.

Self-management in teal-coloured organizations is about **trusting** one another, realizing an open form of **information sharing and business management**, and creating **full responsibility and accountability** in regard to one other. In addition, we experience that we are all of **equal value** to the organization based on our own unique contribution; we have a **safe and caring workplace**; we understand that we are all connected to one another and therefore see **no separation** between ourselves and others; we can and will continue to **learn** constantly, with each challenge being seen as an opportunity to learn together; and finally, we **resolve conflict** and critically look at ourselves to facilitate change.

Eight basic principles

Trust
- Dealings with each other are based on the assumption that people have positive intentions.
- We trust our colleagues, until given reason not to do so.
- Freedom and responsibility are two sides of the same coin.

Information and decision making
- All company information is open to everyone.
- Each of us is capable of dealing with difficult and sensitive news.
- We believe in the power of collective intelligence. No individual is as smart as everyone. Therefore, all decisions will be made using the advisory process.

Responsibility and accountability
- We all bear full responsibility for the organization. When we feel that something needs to be done, we have a duty to do something about it.
- It is unacceptable to limit our concerns merely to those tasks assigned to us by our role.
- Everyone should feel comfortable holding others accountable for their obligations through feedback and respectful confrontation.

Equivalence
- We are all fundamentally of equal worth.
- At the same time, our community is most valuable when everyone is able to contribute in a distinctive way and when the differences in roles, education, background, interests, skills, characters, perspectives, and so on are appreciated.

Safe and caring workplace

- Any situation can be approached either from a position of fear and separation or from love and connection. We choose love and connection.
- We strive to emotionally and spiritually create safe environments in which each of us can behave in an authentic way.
- We honour moods and states of mind (love, care, recognition, gratitude, curiosity, joy, playfulness, etc.)
- We feel comfortable using words such as 'care', 'love', 'service', 'purpose', and 'soul' in the workplace.

Overcoming separation

- We strive for a workplace in which we can honour parts of ourselves: the cognitive, physical, emotional, and spiritual; the rational and the intuitive; and the feminine and the masculine.
- We recognize that we are all deeply connected, part of a greater whole including all nature and forms of life.

To learn

- Every problem provides an invitation to learn and grow. We will always be learning and we will never be finished learning.
- Failure always remains a possibility. We openly discuss our mistakes and learn from them; hiding or failing to learn from failure is unacceptable.
- Feedback and respectful confrontation are gifts we can share to help one another grow.
- We focus more on strengths than we do on weaknesses, and we focus more on opportunities than we focus on problems.

Relationships and conflicts

- It is impossible to change other people.
- We can only change ourselves.
- We take responsibility for our thoughts, beliefs, words, and actions.
- We do not spread rumours.
- We do not talk about anyone behind their back.
- We resolve one-on-one disagreements and do not drag other people into these problems.
- We do not blame others without considering our own accountability.
- When we are at fault, we take this as an invitation to think about how we might be part of the problem (as well as part of a possible solution).

We can see that trust is an important factor among and according to these principles, one that turns up again and again in regard to the achievement and realization of cooperation and engagement. I will therefore explain and elaborate on this element in greater detail.

Trust as the basis for a positive culture

> *Trust is kind of this economic lubricant. When trust is high, morale is high ... Higher*
> *trust environments produce individuals who are happier.*
> – Paul J. Zak (1962), American neuroeconomist

Trust is one of the most important factors those occasions on which employees assess a leader as being both positive and effective. Trust also helps bring about a positive form of cooperation. Trust offers three basic elements: it makes life predictable, it creates a sense of community, and it provides a good basis for cooperation. Research by the American neuroeconomist Paul Zak, indicates that there is a big difference between so-called low trust organizations and high trust organizations.[63]

Compared with workers from average organizations, employees of high trust organizations reported:

74% less stress	106% more energy
13% less sick leave	50% higher productivity
76% higher engagement	29% greater satisfaction with their life
40% less burnout	

Paul Zak spent years researching how organizations can improve their performance, and came to the following conclusion: the key to better performance mainly lies in developing a culture of trust and the development of meaningfulness because that is how you ensure happiness at work. Happy employees are much more productive and innovative compared with their unhappy colleagues. This led to the development of the following formula:

happiness at work = trust x meaningfulness.

Zak points out that our challenge is to create a culture of *high trust*, one in which the 'production' of the cuddly hormone oxytocin is stimulated and encouraged.

> *Oxytocin is a neuropeptide that functions as a hormone and neurotransmitter. It appears to play an important role in linking social connections with feelings of pleasure. (Source: Wikipedia).*

'If you treat me well, I will also treat you well' is the basis for the initiation of such reciprocity. Oxytocin is produced under conditions of trust, inclusive of all those positive organizational effects as described by Zak. Figure 4.3 shows the model for organizational trust, as developed by Zak.

Through his research, Zak has identified eight factors that function as building blocks for creating a high-trust organizational culture.[64] These concern organizational and leadership interventions, and form the acronym OXYTOCIN: Ovation, eXpectation, Yield, Transfer, Openness, Caring, Invest, and Natural (see the box below).

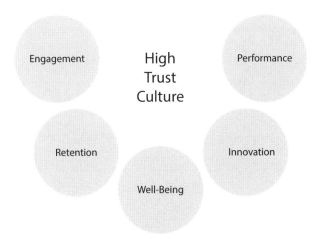

Figure 4.3: Paul Zak: Organizational trust model. (Source: Zak, 2017)

Zak's eight building blocks for creating a high-trust organization

Ovation: Recognizing and acknowledging each other's contribution within the organization. Actively thanking and rewarding is constructive.
Expectation: Experiencing common and difficult-but-achievable challenges, and actively sharing and experiencing these challenges with one another.
Yield: Yielding space and autonomy and realizing objectives.
Transfer: Self-managing of the tasks through the recognition of expertise.
Openness: Sharing information with everyone, which renders listening and communicating important skills.

Caring: Working on relationships with your colleagues.
Invest: Investing in the development of people.
Natural: We are all human, and we all behave in an honest and vulnerable man-
ner. Accordingly. leaders should take responsibility for mistakes made.

There is much at stake. As a leader you want people to trust you and your organization. However, creating this trust – or perhaps more importantly, restoring trust – is not always that easy. Using their 360-degree feedback scores, Zenger and Folkman identify the three main clusters of items that they believe form the basis of trust. They looked at correlations between the trust ratings and selected the 15 highest correlations, after which they performed a factor analysis on these correlations. The outcome showed three clusters of elements: **creating positive relationships**, having **good judgment**, and showing **consistent behaviour** (see the box below).

The basis of trust: Zenger and Folkman's trifecta

1. Positive relationships
Trust is partially based on the extent of a leader's ability to build positive relati-
onships with other people and groups. To create trust, a leader must:
– Stay alert to potential problems and concerns of employees.
– Focus on result-oriented outcomes, but at the same time also be relation-
  oriented.
– Stimulate collaboration.
– Resolve conflicts.
– Provide feedback in an honest and useful way.

2. Good judgement
To be able to trust a leader, a leader must first of all have the right knowledge and be well-informed. A leader must understand the technical aspects of the job and have experience in the discipline concerned. This entails the follo-
wing:
– Leaders use common sense when making decisions.
– Employees trust the leader's opinions and ideas.
– Employees are eager to hear their leader's opinion.
– The knowledge/expertise of the leader makes an important contribution to
  achieving results.
– The leader can quickly anticipate and respond to problems.

3. Consistency

The last element of trust involves saying what you do and doing what you say.

Employees rate a leader highly for trustworthiness if they:

- Function as a role model and lead by example.
- Act according to their words.
- Fulfil their commitments and promises.
- Shows willingness to go beyond what needs to be done.

By understanding the behaviour that underlies trust you, as a leader, will have an improved ability when it comes to increasing this trust.

Zenger and Folkman also analysed the interaction between the three elements of trust. They compared the slightly higher scores (above the 60th percentile) per cluster, and the slightly lower scores (below the 40th percentile) to further investigate the impact on the three elements of trust. The analysis showed that performing just above the norm in each element can lead to substantially positive effects and that, conversely, performing just below the norm can lead to major negative effects regarding the overall trust relationship (see Figure 4.4). Furthermore, the study also showed that general level of trust is strongly related to the way in which people assess their leader's general effectiveness.

The question remains, of course, as to whether you should score higher on all three elements of trust in order to achieve a high level of trust in general. Alternatively, perhaps one particular element has the greatest effect on trust? To investigate this question, Zenger and Folkman conducted an experiment in which leaders were distinguished based on low and high scores for all three elements. The overall level of trust was then considered.

Having positive relationships was found to have the greatest impact on trust. If a leader scored high on consistency and judgement, but low on positive relationships, their trust level dropped by 33 points. Therefore, we see that leaders are also allowed to be inconsistent on occasion. We all find ourselves in situations wherein we plan to do things, but not get around to doing them or else forget to do them. Once a relationship has become damaged or neglected, it is difficult to (again) achieve a high level of trust.

From this research it is interesting to see that focusing on only one of the clusters of trust (as described in the box above) is not enough to create trust. This finding is in contrast to the approach generally advocated by Zenger and Folkman, whereby the focus for achieving leadership effectiveness is placed on the power of a single strength. For trust it is very important that, at the very least, you score well on all three elements; if the scores on all

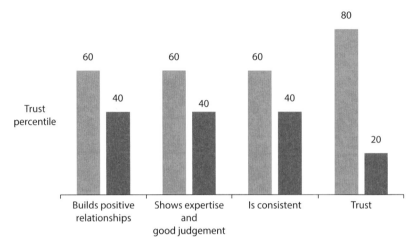

Figure 4.4: The trifecta of trust according to research by Zenger and Folkman. (Source: *Harvard Business Review*, 2019)

three are above the 60th percentile, we see high trust scores among these leaders. This led the researchers to call these three elements **the trifecta of trust**.

Summary: We can see and determine that the challenge for any leader is to create an engaged team. For this it is important to understand the impact you have on the team. Every leader – and every professional – is 'contagious' in regard to their behaviour and emotions, both positive and negative. Creating a positive work culture is essential here. Leading people to achieve better results is not a matter of structure but of culture, whereby trust in the leader is an essential condition.

In the next chapter, the concept of culture will be further identified and determined, providing insights into the possibility of actually transforming your organization.

Confucius | 551 BCE–479 BCE

Niccolò Machiavelli | 1469-1527

Thomas Carlyle | 1795-1881

Frederick Taylor | 1856-1915

Max Weber | 1864-1920

Bertrand Russell | 1872-1970

Simone de Beauvoir | 1908-1986

Abraham Maslow | 1908-1970

Peter Drucker | 1909-2005 — *Culture eats strategy for breakfast.*

John W. Gardner | 1912-2002

Nelson Mandela | 1918-2013

Thomas Kuhn | 1922-1996

Jim Rohn | 1930-2009

Jack Zenger | 1931

Umberto Eco | 1932-2016

Jack Welch | 1935-2020 — *If you want to change the culture of an organization, change the way it develops its leaders*

Richard Petty | 1937

Jesse Jackson | 1941

Stephen Kern | 1943

Daniel Goleman | 1946

Anders Ericsson | 1947-2020

John C. Maxwell | 1947

Peter Senge | 1947

Jaap van Muijen | 1960

Otto Scharmer | 1961

Paul J. Zak | 1962

Frederic Laloux | 1969

5. Transforming the organization

Culture eats strategy for breakfast.
– Peter Drucker (1909–2005), American writer, professor, and consultant in disciplines such as organizational theory and management.

In 2016 it was announced that Twitter's share prices had stagnated considerably, and the company experienced its lowest-ever closing price. Despite this setback, something remarkable happened. Twitter employees praised the company through tweets and frequently used the hashtag #OneTeam. Even in times of uncertainty and challenge, Twitter employees remained enthusiastic about the organization's vision and mission. These tweets showed that employees felt part of the organization, and that they had contributed to a greater good.[65] This feeling is very important, and serves as an incentive for achieving organizational goals.

The careers website Glassdoor has studied feedback ratings from thousands of employees and reported that Twitter received their highest employee rating in the area of organizational culture. But what makes Twitter's organizational culture so attractive to work in? According to Glassdoor's research, three themes repeatedly emerged from the employee comments:
1. The organization has an important mission.
2. The organization acts with care for integrity.
3. Employees feel as if they have found a 'second family' in the company.

Organizational cultures are a collection of norms, values, and behavioural expressions that are shared by the members of an organization, and which bind these members to one another and to the organization itself. An organizational culture can express itself in externalities and in deeply felt values. (Source: Wikipedia)

Culture as leverage

When it comes to influencing human thinking and behaviour, culture is an incredibly powerful force. Within organizations, culture is promoted through the transfer of group norms and leadership. Our culture tells us what is 'good' and 'bad'. We like to belong to a group because the group serves as a frame of reference for how we should or should not behave – this dynamic makes us feel connected.

Every person belongs to one or more groups; think of groups of friends, family, nationality, or the organization in which you work. Culture plays an important role concerning our norms and values, not only in regard to their formation but also in their expression. It is important that employees are able to develop themselves within an organization. They develop themselves on the basis of targeted positive/reinforcing feedback (see Chapter 6) which stems from trust and integrity, incorporating clear and feasible challenge with a conscious contribution of expertise; the result of this is that organizational objectives are achieved.[66] These are all important ingredients for a shared organizational culture.

Unfortunately, many leaders do not yet recognize the added value that can be created through a stimulating organizational culture. When promoting a high-performing culture (see Chapter 3), it is important that leadership focuses on the continuous development of all the people within the organization, something that also changes as a result. De Waal's five success factors, and the mutual dynamics between these factors, provide a good insight into the connection between leadership and the organization as a whole. De Waal's conclusion from his 2013 research is that leadership is the determining factor for success.[67] Leadership determines the culture of the organization, whereby the people within the organization can make a successful contribution to organizational goals.

Academica BV (a recognized training and knowledge centre for directors, leaders, and professionals) has translated this for its students into the dynamics of effective leadership with the total environment, in which the autonomous professional in a developing organization is the starting point (see Figure 5.1). This model serves as the basis for the process of change at, for example, an educational institution transforming into a high performing school.

Scientific research has shown a direct correlation between a healthy, productive organizational culture and organizational results. Despite this, many leaders spend most of their time organizing the right strategy without considering the effect of culture. Every organization has a certain strategy, but before this strategy is implemented, careful thought must be given to the mission, vision, and core values of the organization itself. Think of questions such as: What does our organization aim to convey to our customers? What is the added value of our organization at the present time? What should our employees stand for and believe in when they work for our organization? Strategy and organizational culture are inextricably linked, and should not be seen as independent elements.

Figure 5.1: High performing organizations and the dynamics of leadership. (Source: Academica BV, 2020)

The formal logic behind this process is strategy, which provides clarity for both collective action and decision-making. While leadership goes hand in hand with strategy, development culture, on the other hand, is seen by many leaders as a less tangible phenomenon. Culture is anchored in unspoken behaviour, ways of thinking and social patterns, or – as we often call them – **'the unwritten rules of the game'**. This often results in the influence of culture becoming greater; but this does not mean that it is any less important. The right organizational culture acts as a lever in the realization of the strategy, and leadership is central to the right organizational culture.[68]

This chapter started with a quote from Peter Drucker: 'Culture eats strategy for breakfast.' With this, Drucker indicates that, regardless of the organizational strategy you try to implement or pursue, its success and effectiveness will still be determined by the culture in which employees are implementing and carrying out that strategy.

Culture and leadership, as we can see, are inextricably linked. It is leaders who determine the norms and values and, therefore, the strength of an organizational culture. The mantra of the famous Dutch football manager, Louis Van Gaal – 'It is not the best players who win, but the best team' – is a good example of this sentiment. As a trainer-coach, this was Van Gaal's focus. Accordingly, the team always comes first, and no individual is more important than the whole. Any individual who failed to understand this concept did not fit into his team. The fact that 'as a player you can play a perfect match, and still lose as a team', is indisputable.

It is important that leaders do not view focus on organizational culture as something secondary. When leaders fail to understand the power, dynamics, and contagiousness of a culture, the organization's plans and objectives will never be effectively achieved. Culture is the tacit social ordering of an organization, and the shaping of its attitudes, relationships, and behaviours in a sustainable way. The norms within an organization define what behaviour is encouraged, discouraged, accepted, or rejected. When a culture is properly aligned with personal values, motivations, and needs within an organization, it can generate tremendous energy in employees to work towards a common goal.

To change the organizational culture, the leader must also change

If you want to change the culture of an organization, change the way it develops its leaders.
– Jack Welch (1935), American business executive,
CEO of General Electric, and author

The studies of John Kotter (1947) and James Heskett (1933), both professors at Harvard University, have given us important new insights into thinking about leadership, organizational culture, and change management. Kotter has studied the actions of leaders for over 30 years and his book *Leading Change*, in which he describes eight factors that lead to the successful implementation of change within organizations, is a bestseller.[69] In summary, Kotter distinguishes three stages of movement within the process of change: creating a climate of success, involving the people in the movement, and supporting the implementation of that movement.

Heskett and Kotter co-wrote the book *Corporate Culture and Performance*.[70] In their study of 200 organizations, Heskett and Kotter conclude that organizations that are able to easily adapt to their culture (*agility*) will experience higher financial returns. When researchers look at changing organizations and their leaders, we see that culture – involving people in the change process – is always a success determining factor (see also the previous chapter about impact on the team).

The present zeitgeist is increasingly focused on continuous change and innovation. Organizations must constantly improve in order to maintain their competitive advantage and remain sustainable. Leaders have a duty to engage employees in this regard. However, we see that organizations often realize this too late and/or that their initiatives for implementing change fail. It turns out that it is very difficult for many organizations to implement new processes for new activities and behaviours.

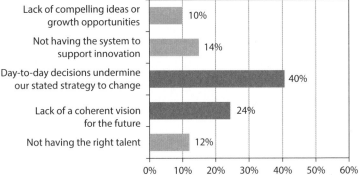

Figure 5.2: A graphical representation of Innosight's research into organizational culture. (Source: Anthony et al., 2016)

A study among the leaders of 91 organizations – from more than 20 sectors and with revenues over 1 billion USD – was conducted by the consulting firm Innosight. The study posed the following question: What is the biggest obstacle facing an organization when transforming its culture in response to a market change?[71] Overall, 40 per cent of the respondents indicated the biggest hurdle to be: *daily decisions that undermine the strategy*. The next most common popular answer, at 24 per cent, was: *a lack of a coherent vision for the future* (see Figure 5.2).

The consequences for organizations that find it difficult to adapt and that are, therefore, not *agile*, is illustrated by the Fortune 500 list – a ranking of companies from the United States according to their annual turnover. In 1955, organizations on the Fortune 500 list had been on the list for an average of 75 years; today, this has fallen to 14.5 years. Globalization and digitization have accelerated our society, and organizations must continue to follow the pace of change in order to survive and maintain a competitive advantage. These developments have an impact on organizations as well as on the positions they occupy. It is very important that organizations know how to be *agile* with a human touch in order to guarantee social security and success (see also the convergence of fast and qualitative action described earlier in Chapter 3).

There are various options for changing the organizational culture; however, one important aspect is often forgotten: '**If you want to change the**

culture of an organization, change the way it develops its leaders'. This is an important insight into changing organizational cultures as provided by Jack Welch.

As was made clear through the contributions of Senge and Scharmer in Chapter 1, leadership development concerns the development of everyone within an organization. Only in this way does development influence processes of change. The biggest challenge is not that change must be carried out by the leader, but that it must be carried out by *everyone* within the organization; the success of the organization depends on a large number of individuals. Successful leadership development values both individual and organizational development. Leadership development itself is the process through which employees and leaders are intertwined, and whereby a natural connection and interaction takes place. The definition of leadership introduced in Chapter 1 is therefore emphasized once again.

> *Leadership is the behaviour that elevates individual performance and drives superior organizational outcomes.*

Using this definition we understand that, first of all, leadership is present at all levels of the organization – it has an influence in all layers. Secondly, we understand that it must be clear to everyone what the organization's goals are, and what this means for the work of the individual. Organizational change and the achievement and maximization of objectives is a common process, and one that everyone in the organization can contribute to (see Laloux's previously described work). By organizing and enabling leadership development at every level of the organization, the development of the organization as a whole is facilitated. Collaboration is based on norms, standards, and explicit values. The desired direction and the speed with which the organization must change according to these principles is crystal clear to everyone.

Leadership development and the development of an organizational culture cannot be viewed independently. Research by Emmanuel Ogbonna and Lloyd C. Harris provides empirical evidence that a leadership style influences the culture of an organization.[72] Organizational culture affects the performance of that organization through leadership, while the development of leadership and the development of an organizational culture are a connected pair, and constantly reinforce one another. In other studies these two elements, shown together in Figure 5.3, have always been analysed separately: leadership and its effect on organizational results, or culture and its effect on organizational results. In this study, the three elements have been viewed together. This gives the impression that they are dynamically connected to one another.

Figure 5.3: The relationship between leadership, organizational culture, and organizational outcomes. (Source: Ogbonna & Harris, 2000)

In order to influence the culture of an organization, it is important to develop its leaders. The process of development is not only concerned with the formal leader, but must be carefully implemented at all levels of the organization so that everyone can be included in the change. Unfortunately, initiatives for change and development are not always successful. It is therefore good to consider what we can do better together to make leadership development activities more successful.

Leadership development: three points for improvement

In my work as an organizational consultant and mentor of leaders in different types of organizations, I repeatedly see the same pitfalls – which can develop into success factors – in making the improvement process for leaders really work. It is essential that development is not seen as a separate process from the leader in question. The leader's manager should also be involved in the process of development. One does not develop on one's own. In addition, I see that many people think that if they register for a leadership development course, they immediately initiate their development. However, you mainly develop yourself in your daily work practice, and so your development should also express itself there accordingly. The impact of your behaviour, each and every day, makes the difference, not what you do or say at home or during a course. Finally, we see that the follow-up to the process of development is often not supplied with a 'breeding ground'. The application of what was learned in the course turns out to be more challenging than expected.

A positive example of how the application of leadership development can be carried out can be seen in a certain secondary education foundation, which has fully implemented the core elements of the leadership programme in all their professionalization activities. Development discussions are conducted on the basis of the CPO model provided (see Chapter 2). The professionals at this institute use this analysis model to formulate concrete actions and to continuously evaluate and adjust them. The HR staff is supportive of both personal coaching as well as the systems used. Leaders all know the theoretical starting points and apply these theoretical principles themselves and through these support their own teams. The 360-degree feedback is organized centrally within this foundation every year, and new employees are immediately included in this development approach through training. The director is proud that the entire HR system is geared towards continuous learning together and that the organization is therefore always taking positive steps in regard to its common development.

The three elements of leadership development

Involve managers in the development process

Research by Zenger and Folkman conducted among 61 leaders within the financial sector, revealed the following.[73] Leaders were asked to describe their manager's level of support for their development plan. These levels of support were divided into three groups: non-supportive managers, somewhat supportive managers, and highly supportive managers. Thereafter these leaders were asked to describe the progress they had made in their development plans by responding according to a four-point Linkert-type scale, 'I feel that I have made progress in improving the specific issues in my development plan'. Those who indicated 'Agree' or 'Strongly Agree' were referred to as 'Improvers'. Zenger and Folkman found that leaders with highly supportive managers were more than twice as likely to think they had improved than leaders with non-supportive managers.

In other words: if you send your people on a training course, but are not involved in their development, you are better just giving them a dinner coupon!

Implement development in your work

Many mistakenly assume that there is a barrier between daily work and personal development. Conscientious employees almost always put their work first and invariably delay personal development until they 'find time' or 'have a break'. As a result, personal development almost always comes second and job performance comes first. However, daily work-related activities should go hand in hand with personal development; in this way a lever is created in which personal development will yield better work results. Our personal development allows us to become better members of the organization and will improve the overall performance of the organization.

The goal of (personal) development is not to learn something for yourself, you develop so that you can use your improvement in knowledge and skills for your own working environment, and thus create a greater impact. Personal development ensures higher employee engagement and greater job satisfaction.

Define development concepts that are implemented in all HR systems

The competencies selected for the development of the professional as a leader must concern their impact on the organization. These competencies and goals should therefore not be formulated solely through the focus of the leader's development. We often see HR departments being set up and developed as separate entities, separate from the primary process. We can only make the connection between development and the organization when goals for development are embedded in the selection, the performance management, and the rewards and the objectives of all employees. Only then can we jointly bring about organizational development. In short, goals for leadership development must be translated into organizational goals.

Innovative culture

> *Innovation requires willing to be misunderstood for long periods of time.*
> – Jeff Bezos (1964), CEO of Amazon

Jeff Bezos, CEO of Amazon and the richest man in the world, is fixated on the future and tries to focus as little as possible on the present. He is known for working 2 or 3 years ahead of the present time, and most of his leadership team adopts the same mindset. Accordingly, Bezos focuses on what customers will need in the future. After starting Amazon in his garage, Bezos initially only sold books; today, he sells almost everything – indeed, Amazon has since become the largest trading company on the Internet. Bezos' mantra – 'innovation requires long-term willingness to be misunderstood' – exactly describes that phenomenon which prevents many leaders from successfully bringing about innovation. Such leaders prefer to 'play it safe'. They emphasize short-term pressures, and indicate that innovation is a vague and ambiguous concept and is therefore difficult to implement. However, we live in an era in which innovation has become a strategic necessity for organizations, and innovation itself is seen as one of the most important characteristics of successful organizations. Innovative leaders provide and generate impulses and generate ideas, ensuring that an organization continues to develop, and that it can respond dynamically to changes in the environment and future needs. Jos de Blok, the founder of Buurtzorg – an innovator in the home-care sector mentioned in Laloux's book as an example of a teal-coloured organization – took the initiative and undertook a complete overhaul of his healthcare firm. He decided he would no longer be in charge of all decisions within his organization.

When an organization is to be transformed, many organization experience the incentive to do so in an innovative way. In the article 'Stimulating innovative work behaviour in organizations: an overview of empirical findings', Frederik Anseel and Toon Devloo discuss those factors influencing innovative work behaviour.[74] This article uses the definition of innovative behaviour provided by West and Farr as a basis.[75] The definition of innovative behaviour according to West and Farr (1990) is:

> 'the intentional introduction and application within a role, group or organization of ideas, processes, products or procedures, new to the relevant unit of adoption designed to significantly benefit the individual, group, organization or wider society.'

The conclusions of the research focus on those ideas and images with which we, as professionals, are confronted as part of our daily practice; however, empirical research puts these ideas and images into perspective, often showing or representing them as myths. Here I shall mention a few points that will sharpen our image of what actually makes innovation possible.

1. **The cognitive skills**

   Extensive knowledge and experience that have been built up over the years, along with necessary and precisely mastered work skills, stimulate and incentivize innovative work behaviour.[76] The research does away with the assumption that is currently seen a lot in the education sector regarding the application of so-called new learning; specifically, that people who are new to a certain domain can and will automatically be innovative and creative because they are unhindered by stereotypical thinking patterns and set procedures.

2. **Personality**

   When studying the five personality traits (see Chapter 1), as identified by psychologists over time, we see that within them 'openness' is the main stimulator of innovative work behaviour. Also important are the ability to deal with uncertainty, a high-degree of self-confidence, and a proactive attitude.

3. **Motivation**

   The study does away with the idea that only a positive attitude from the leader is enough to work well (to ensure innovative behaviour). It is precisely when under pressure and with the right support from the manager that innovative leaders are seen to emerge.

4. **Team climate**

   It is essential that there is a common vision. In addition, the degree to which the team participates rate is organized is also of great importance. Do I have influence and a say in the process? In addition, it is crucial that there is support and that there are norms that make change possible. Conflicts have a negative effect on the process of change and are therefore not stimulating.

5. **Team processes**

   The manner in which communication takes place both internally and externally is very important, and it must be possible to 'cut the Gordian knot', even if there are people in the group who are still set against a certain decision. The so-called integration skills are essential for a team in order to spread vision and knowledge within and outside of the team.

6. **Leadership**

   An open attitude and the generation of trust are important behaviours of the leader. But more interestingly, we see that transformational leadership (the motivational leadership style based on a vision of the future, inspiration, and intellectual stimulation) has a greater impact on driving innovative work behaviour than transactional leadership (a leadership style based on responding to the needs of team members, providing structures, and not intervening so long as nothing is going wrong).[77]

The conclusions of Anseel and Devloo's research are in line with Zenger and Folkman's research on the behaviours of highly effective leaders who pursue and encourage innovation within their organizational cultures.[78] Innovation is about the individual's, the team's, and the organization's contributions to society. The ten important factors that emerged from Zenger and Folkman's research concerning this subject are:

1. **Excellent strategic vision**

   Leaders display an excellent strategic vision for the future and often ask themselves the following question: *Is there a better way?* The employees of these leaders indicate that these leaders excel in painting a clear picture for the future.

2. **Customer-oriented focus**
   These leaders never lose sight of one thing: the importance of customer focus. Customers help you to become successful and therefore the focus should be on them. These leaders have a large social network and are constantly wondering how they can respond to customer's needs and wishes.

3. **Climate of reciprocal trust**
   Innovative leaders trust their team members and allow their employees to act autonomously, thereby creating a sense of security, which makes employees more trustful of their leaders. In addition, employees of innovative leaders are never punished for mistakes they admit to.

4. **Loyalty to doing what is right for the organization and the customer**
   These leaders are not afraid to go against the hierarchy. They are willing to tackle difficult issues, to disagree with individuals from higher levels within the organization, and to solve problems that actually belong to other organizations. In addition, they are never afraid to contradict contemporary views.

5. **Culture that stimulates upward communication**
   These leaders recognize the importance of communication and know that communication should not always take place at the top of the organization's hierarchy. They are aware that employees with direct customer contact best understand where innovation needs to take place and what needs to change.

6. **Are persuasive**
   These leaders present new ideas with conviction and enthusiasm: they do not force their views on others, but rather promote contagion among others with their positive emotions.

7. **Stretch goals**
   These leaders set stretch goals, and these goals require their employees to go further than merely working harder; it requires employees to find new ways to achieve their targets.

8. **Focus on speed**
   These leaders have a sense of urgency, and are aware they must do things quickly as well as doing things well. Fast experiments are an important key to successful innovations. For example, the prototype of Google's email service was created in a single day.

9. **Are candid in their communication**
   These leaders provide honest and sincere feedback. Employees experience that they can always count on honest answers from their leader.

10. **Inspire and motivate through action**

These leaders excel at inspiring others; they have a clear sense of purpose and what meaning their work has. Furthermore, they are able to convey the right positive energy. Think of constructive speeches from great leaders, such as Barack Obama's mantra, 'Yes We Can'.

Summary: We can therefore conclude that it is important for leaders to understand the dynamics and emotional contagion of an organizational culture in order for a transformation of that organization to take place successfully. Consider once more that organizational strategy must be combined with cultural norms and values. Cultural change within an organization means leadership development at all levels and layers, and is therefore about the development of the organization as a whole. In order to guarantee its ongoing existence it is important that you, as a leader, keep your organization agile in regard to the human and personal dimension. Therefore, try to involve professionals within the organization in your development process, combine your daily work tasks with your personal development and translate this into the organizational objectives. Innovation is an indispensable factor for improving organizations. However, to work on these, choose those behaviours that can enhance the strength and sustainability of the organization.

We need the fuel of feedback in order to start and sustain our development. Therefore, in the upcoming chapter we will further investigate the process of giving feedback, how the process works, and what always prevents us from doing this frequently and doing it well.

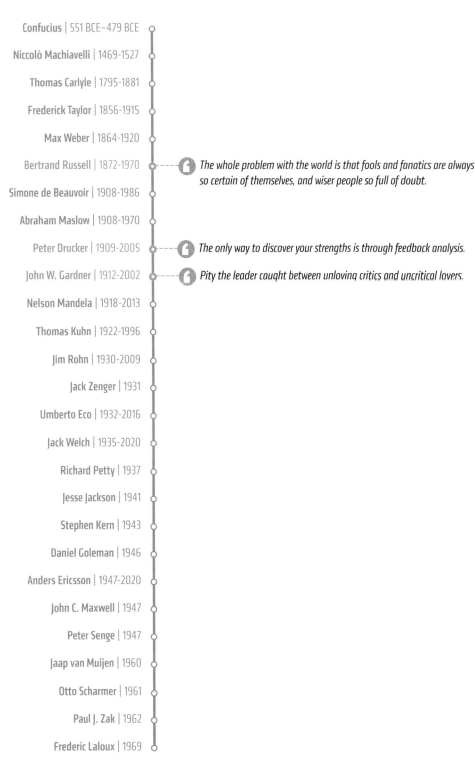

Confucius | 551 BCE–479 BCE

Niccolò Machiavelli | 1469-1527

Thomas Carlyle | 1795-1881

Frederick Taylor | 1856-1915

Max Weber | 1864-1920

Bertrand Russell | 1872-1970 — *The whole problem with the world is that fools and fanatics are always so certain of themselves, and wiser people so full of doubt.*

Simone de Beauvoir | 1908-1986

Abraham Maslow | 1908-1970

Peter Drucker | 1909-2005 — *The only way to discover your strengths is through feedback analysis.*

John W. Gardner | 1912-2002 — *Pity the leader caught between unloving critics and uncritical lovers.*

Nelson Mandela | 1918-2013

Thomas Kuhn | 1922-1996

Jim Rohn | 1930-2009

Jack Zenger | 1931

Umberto Eco | 1932-2016

Jack Welch | 1935-2020

Richard Petty | 1937

Jesse Jackson | 1941

Stephen Kern | 1943

Daniel Goleman | 1946

Anders Ericsson | 1947-2020

John C. Maxwell | 1947

Peter Senge | 1947

Jaap van Muijen | 1960

Otto Scharmer | 1961

Paul J. Zak | 1962

Frederic Laloux | 1969

6. Feedback as an engine for development

The whole problem with the world is that fools and fanatics are always so certain of themselves, and wiser people so full of doubts.
– Bertrand Russell (1872–1970), philosopher, mathematician, historian, writer, and Nobel Prize winner in Literature

Most people think they know themselves better than any other person ever could. Self-evaluations and self-assessments methods are therefore widely used by organizations to gain insight into ways people act. However, as early as 1923 it was shown by G.J. Hoffman that self-assessments are limited in their reliability;[79] the limited reliability of self-assessments has since been confirmed many times by other researchers.[80] Indeed, self-evaluations prove to be unreliable, inaccurate, and *biased*.[81] Self-reflection is, in fact, not as truthful as the person doing the self-reflection often thinks. In psychology, this is referred to as the *Dunning–Kruger effect*: incompetent people overestimate their own abilities, while people who actually perform above average often underestimate themselves and assume that other people are just as capable as they are.

The Dunning–Kruger effect also emerged in a research study conducted by Zenger and Folkman,[82] which used a cohort of 69,000 leaders. From this study it was found that the most effective leaders underestimated themselves (see Figure 6.1). These leaders continuously strive for better performance.

In the same study, it was found that those leaders who 'undervalue' themselves had more engaged employees (see Figure 6.2). This idea can easily be illustrated: just picture someone who always brags about themselves, someone who feels superior and always feels the need to share their achievements with other people. When confronted with people such as these we tend to avoid them; we think of them as arrogant, and are therefore less likely to assume that they are competent. Conversely, we value modest people. We enjoy working for a leader who is competent, but not self-absorbed.

A study conducted in 2003 found another notable result when investigating students at Cornell University.[83] In this study, which was conducted by psychologists David Dunning and Joyce Ehrlinger it was found that, when asked to estimate their performance on test scores within their own discipline, the female students were more likely to underestimate themselves, while their male colleagues were more likely to overestimated themselves. However, no quantitative or qualitative difference could be found between

Comparing self-ratings to results from 360-degree surveys.

<small>LEADERSHIP EFFECTIVENESS RATING, IN PERCENTILE</small>

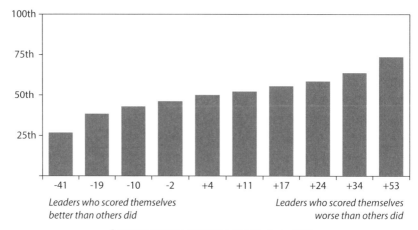

Figure 6.1: The most effective leaders underestimate themselves. (Source: *Harvard Business Review*, Zenger & Folkman, 2015)

Comparing self-ratings to results from 360-degree surveys.

<small>EMPLOYEE ENGAGEMENT RATING, IN PERCENTILE</small>

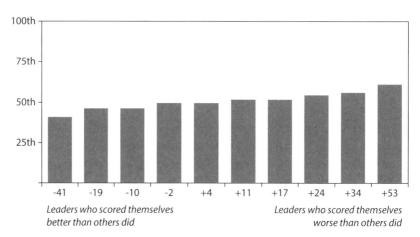

Figure 6.2: Leaders who underestimate themselves have more engaged employees. (Source: *Harvard Business Review*, Zenger & Folkman, 2015)

these two groups regarding their actual performance (for more information on the impact of the differences between men and women, see Chapter 8).

Therefore we can see and conclude that it is quite difficult to reflect on and assess oneself correctly. Accordingly, we need other people to break our own bias!

Feedback: because you are worth it

> *The only way to discover your strengths is through feedback analysis.*
> – Peter Drucker (1909–2005), American writer, professor, and consultant, in areas such as organizational theory and management.

Feedback adds enormous value to your development process. Friends, family, employees, and colleagues can help you in this process, as they may recognize certain behaviours that you may be less aware of without their help. Goethe's German saying 'Was sich liebt, das neckt sich' ('that which loves one another, teases one another') has a special meaning for many.

Sooner or later, each of us will have to deal with feedback throughout our professional careers. In large corporations, feedback procedures often belong to so-called standard operating procedures, but small and medium-sized organizations are often still looking for the best means by which they can incorporate and utilize feedback. Most professionals and organizations do not know how to organize feedback and get the most use out of it. The result of providing and asking for too little feedback is that there is no focus on continuous improvement. Learning to give feedback as well as receive feedback are both essential skills for professionals; both are necessary to optimize your effectiveness as a professional and to enable and bring about a continuously learning organization. There are plenty of reasons for further investigating and interpreting the process of giving feedback, the benefits this process provides, as well as the uncertainties that it might entail.

Within the feedback process, two core human needs are touched upon (see also the starting principles for teal-coloured organizations according to Laloux in Chapter 4):
1. The need to learn and grow.
2. The need to be accepted for who you are.

First, let us consider the origin of the word 'feedback' and what it actually means. Feedback stems from the Old English word *fedan*, meaning 'to feed'

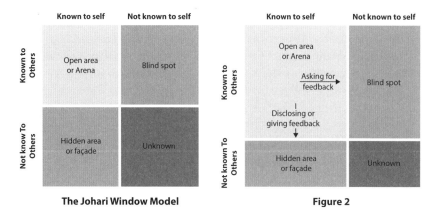

Figure 6.3: The Johari window. (Source: Communication theory)

or 'to nourish'. **Feedback** therefore literally means '**to feed back**'. In other words, feedback means providing information to a person about the way their behaviour comes across and whether it is properly understood. The definition of feedback I would like to share is:

> *Feedback: Information possessed by someone else which they decide to share with you because they feel that you are not fully aware of it and that, if you were, you might benefit from it.*

The Johari Window (see Figure 6.3), developed by Joseph Luft and Harry Ingham, provides insight into different aspects and areas of our personality to be discovered, as well as the need to become aware of these aspects and areas.[84] The model describes the challenges in our personal development within the context in which we find ourselves on a day-to-day basis.

The four domains to be discovered are: **what we know about ourselves; what we don't know about ourselves; what others know about us**; and finally, **what others don't know about us**.

The four domains in this model clearly show where giving and receiving feedback appeals to our own awareness, our ability to develop acceptance in regard to such feedback, and our awareness pertaining to our own personality; however, these four domains also invite those within our environment to learn more about our situation and possibilities and opportunities.

Imagine that you are going to work in a new environment, one in which your new colleagues still know little about the knowledge and skills you have to offer. By asking for feedback from these colleagues you can gain greater insight into your performance (and perhaps find or identify your *blind spot*). But also by giving feedback to your colleagues, you can indicate

where your expertise lies, thereby expanding the so-called *open area/arena*:
the right-hand part of the model in Figure 6.3.

As a general rule it is good to make the open area on the left-hand side
of the model as large as possible. This can be done in two ways:

– By asking for feedback from others, the space shifts from that of the
  blind spot to that of the open area, meaning that the blind spot becomes
  smaller and the open area expands.
– By communicating openly and providing feedback, the space shifts
  from the hidden area to the open space.

When we take a closer look at the definition of feedback, it is difficult to
imagine that asking for, giving, and receiving feedback cause so much stress.
Unfortunately, many leaders and their employees find receiving feedback
an unpleasant experience. How come?

Feedback is perceived as unpleasant

What makes receiving feedback so difficult?
The following points may be recognizable:
   The feedback is personal.
   Emotions can come into play.
   *The significance of the relationship between the feedback giver and the feed-
   back receiver.*
   We don't always agree with the feedback we hear.

What makes giving feedback so difficult?
Here, too, we see the same elements:
   It is difficult to predict someone's response to feedback.
   The conversation could have negative consequences.
   Redirecting feedback may not come across as intended.

Accordingly, we can see that there can be quite a few obstacles to a good
feedback conversation. John Gardner – who is known, among many other
things, for his book *On Leadership* – puts it this way:

> *Pity the leader caught between unloving critics and uncritical lovers.*
> – John W. Gardner (1912–2002), in an opening address at Cornell University in 1968

Nobody wants to receive a continuous stream of negative feedback, but at the
same time no one benefits from ceaseless insincere flattery. In order to keep

being honest with yourself, you need *loving critics*; these people are willing to give the honest feedback you need so that you can become the best leader you can be. The positive thing is that you can stimulate this behaviour in order to facilitate the feedback process, both for yourself and for your employees.

In many organizations we see that a familial feeling or feelings of insecurity creates a barrier to giving honest feedback with complete openness. To foster a learning culture through frequent feedback, you have to consider our human needs and emotions. The elements that make it difficult to give and receive feedback – mentioned in the box above – can be traced back to eight human needs and emotions: predictability, independence, meaning, inclusion, status, fairness, affection, and engagement (see box below).

Predictability

Is it clear what my future will bring? Can I keep predicting what will happen to me and my job/work?

Independence

Can I 'pilot my own ship'? Do I actually have a say in my decisions, and will I be able to continue to make decisions myself?

Meaning

Does what I do make a difference to my team or my organization? Do I know what is ultimately important to me?

Inclusion

Am I involved as a member of my group or team? Do others take me seriously and do I belong there?

Status

Am I respected within this group? Where do I stand in relation to others in the group? Am I moving up or down?

Fairness

Am I treated fairly in comparison to others?

Affection

What is my relationship with others in this group? Are the relationships warm or cool?

Engagement

Am I enthusiastic about what I do, the people I work with and the organization I work for?

Which of these eight human needs and emotions do you recognize, and which do you find particularly important in your work environment? Furthermore, which of these needs and emotions make you feel threatened when you receive feedback about your work or activities/behaviours?

Here, too, we recognize the principles discussed in Chapter 4 in regard to becoming an engaged team together.

Despite good intentions, even the thought of a conversation in which feedback will be given can already cause uncertainty anxiety in some individuals. Feeling threatened and anxious over a feedback session can evoke emotional and physiological responses that hinder the way in which you can have conversations with one another. For feedback to be effective, the anxiety and stress associated with feedback must be reduced as much as possible. It is easier to talk about an open climate in which everyone gives and asks one another for feedback, than it is to actually make this a reality. This transition requires good guidance and a good example.

Feedback: should I ask?

Many leaders mistakenly assume that asking for feedback is a sign of weakness or insecurity. A Zenger and Folkman study of more than 50,000 leaders found that those leaders who actively solicit feedback score higher in regard to leadership effectiveness. Leaders who frequently ask for feedback score, on average, at the 86th percentile in overall leadership effectiveness. Comparatively, leaders who ask for little or no feedback score, on average, at the 15th percentile (see Figure 6.4).

The conscious search for an environment in which you receive feedback (by inviting people to provide you with honest feedback) supports you in your development and in your improvement process. The feedback process therefore starts with you. It is important that inviting other people to provide you with honest feedback is included in your standard action repertoire. It is highly unlikely that employees or colleagues will provide feedback of their own accord, especially if the environment in question does not offer the possibilities to so in a safe and secure manner. As a leader you must therefore set a good example. Let colleagues and employees know that you are open to feedback. Make it clear to them that no negative consequences will result from or will be connected with the feedback process. Furthermore, you should emphasize that honest and reinforcing feedback creates and cultivates a closer and better organizational culture. In this way a norm is created, one whereby feedback is no longer 'terrifying'. Employees who feel free to provide feedback will also feel as if their opinion matters. When asking for feedback as a leader, you are more likely to receive a sincere and honest answer because employees feel heard and recognized.

BETTER LEADERS ASK FOR MORE FEEDBACK

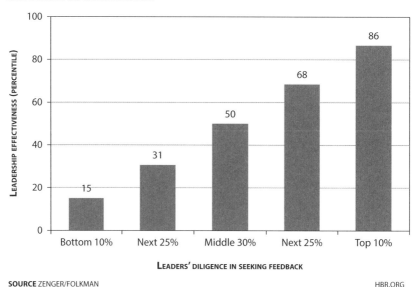

SOURCE ZENGER/FOLKMAN   HBR.ORG

Figure 6.4: Effective leaders ask for more feedback. (Source: *Harvard Business Review*, Zenger & Folkman, 2013)

Responding to feedback: seven principles

While most feedback contains both positive and negative aspects and elements, the feedback receiver often focuses on those weaknesses that need to be improved. However, we know that highly effective leaders do not achieve their status through the absence of weaknesses, but rather because they excel at a number of things. You do not have to be perfect to be a highly effective leader, so long as your weaknesses are not fatal flaws (see Chapter 2). Feedback will have the greatest impact if it ensures that you do not allow weaknesses to grow to a critical point, and if it helps you further develop your competencies in such a way that they become strengths that increase your overall leadership effectiveness. This is more satisfying and provides you with the positive energy to keep going. Finally, remember that *deliberate practice*, as highlighted by Anders Ericsson (Chapter 1), requires considerable perseverance.

A number of principles are important if one is to properly understand how feedback works. In Joe Folkman's book *The Power of Feedback*, 35 individual principles are named and identified.[85] I will now discuss seven of these principles. Furthermore, I invite you to reflect on each of these principles, consider how you have experienced them thus far, and think about what you can do to better accept each principle for yourself.

Principle 1
Asking others to provide feedback increases their expectation that you are willing to change yourself in a positive way.

There are two possible responses to feedback: either you decide to do nothing with the feedback, or you try to convert the feedback into tangible and measurable change goals. The feedback provider will become frustrated if nothing results from the feedback they have given; similarly, the feedback receiver who decides not to act on, or do anything as a result of, the feedback will also become frustrated in the long run. This is because there is no positive dynamic between the feedback giver and the feedback receiver. When you ask for feedback, you indicate that you want to change yourself for the better. Others will take your word for it, but if you do not take the feedback seriously or do anything with it, people will begin to lose faith in you. However, if after asking for feedback you respond constructively to the feedback provided and try to improve your behaviour – and furthermore ask for additional feedback about this issue again at a later date – you will create a feedback culture in which people feel invited to give feedback while also feeling comfortable when doing so.

Principle 2
When you receive feedback but do not improve yourself as a result, your feedback givers will perceive this in a negative way.

Negative or redirecting feedback is often experienced painfully, and we all know that such rejection can feel uncomfortable or even unpleasant. A study by Eisenberger et al. (2003) shows that the brain processes rejection in the same way as it experiences physical pain (see Figure 6.5). It is therefore not illogical that people prefer to avoid feedback so that they can prevent pain or painful experiences. However, you need feedback in order to grow. The process of improving through feedback is not easy; you must genuinely want to work on your personal development, something that often entails a painful confrontation.

Leaders who try to improve themselves based on feedback are more likely to be positively perceived. This is important because having positive relationships with employees provides a positive energy for working together towards important organizational outcomes. However, because it is generally

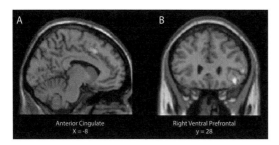

Fig. 1. (A) Increased activity in anterior cingulate cortex (ACC) during exclusion relative to inclusion. **(B)** Increased activity in right ventral prefrontal cortex (RVPFC) during exclusion relative to inclusion.

Figure 6.5: The brain processes rejection in the same way that it experiences physical pain. (Source: Eisenberger et al., 2003)

expected that you will take feedback seriously and that you will endeavour to change accordingly, individuals within your environment will assess you more negatively if you fail to do so.

Principle 3
You will not change if you think that you do not need to adjust your behaviour.

When people receive feedback, they are often confronted with a painful self-evaluation. The first reaction to redirecting or negative feedback is often one of denial; this is because people want to keep a positive image of themselves and remain inviolable in the eyes of others. If you are not convinced by the way other people see you, you will not adjust your behaviour. Comparatively, however, if you do want to improve yourself, it is very important that you are open and receptive to feedback. This process starts with adjusting your behaviour, as behaviour comprises the visible part of an individual's actions and deeds. Accordingly, the feedback process will ensure that you improve yourself and increase your effectiveness both as a leader and as a professional.

Principle 4
The perceptions of others are their reality.

The impressions employees and colleagues form of you as a leader comprises the truth to them at that moment. Assessment and appraisal by other people is valuable because there can be a disparity between the way you see yourself through self-perception and how you come across to other people (see the Johari window model). During our childhood we develop the mechanism of 'denial' in order to protect ourselves from critical or negative views that apply to us. As a result, we often try to rationalize negative feedback.

However, when trying to improve your effectiveness, it is important that you experience feedback positively and that you take and consider the perceptions of others seriously. Even if you are sure that certain people have an inaccurate or incorrect view of you, you must remember that this image nevertheless remains the truth to that particular person at that moment in time. In other words, you are responsible for how other people see you. If you want them to see something different, do not complain, rather, try adjusting your behaviour.

> Principle 5
> *To effectively deal effectively with feedback, you need to reflect carefully and maintain an open attitude.*

When receiving feedback, your attitude towards others is extremely important. When we are more open to receiving feedback, other people who may have feedback for you will therefore be more likely to approach you sooner and with greater readiness. Furthermore, those who are not open to feedback will continue to receive less and less feedback as time goes on. If you want feedback to support you in your development, you will have to reflect carefully and with an open mind. People who give feedback do so according to their own perspective and with good intentions. Try having an open conversation and inviting others to indicate how they see and experience certain things or certain aspects of your behaviour.

> Principle 6
> *We provide feedback according to what we do and what we think based on our own experiences and knowledge.*

It is important to understand that we provide feedback from our own frames of reference. Accordingly, we can better reflect on something that is familiar or known to us than we can on something we do not yet know. In those situations in which you do something involving a new type of behaviour – or that involves a new expression of knowledge or skill – the people around you who experience this may do so differently than you intend them to.

Think of the example of a safari guide. This guide helps you discover wild animals in an environment that may be new to you, but that is well known to them. This process will cost you time and effort if you are to be able to see what the guide sees. For example, consider the case of a safari guide. The guide will take tourists around large nature reserves and help them spot wild animals. The guide understands that tourists do not automatically spot what he sees, as their frames of reference, skills, and learned abilities are different from his. Therefore, he tries to convey to tourists his own frame of references and trains them expediently so that they are then able to spot what he can spot. Since the guide has received training in this, he is able do this in a short period. In conclusion, try to be like the safari guide, they are aware other people look at things differently, but take the time to show them their own frame of reference. You, as a leader, are the safari guide, while members of your team are the tourists.

Principle 7
The process of change starts with accepting feedback.

For you to be able to better accept feedback, it is important that you understand how the image-creation process works; that is, to understand how other individuals form a certain image of you. This allows you to better respond to feedback, as people see your behaviour and not your intentions. It is essential that you use clear and careful communication to help those around you to understand your intentions. In addition, it is important to adjust your behaviour so that it agrees with and reflects your intentions.

Employees want feedback: giving feedback

One of the most difficult tasks for a leader is to give feedback. In a feed-back survey, 7,631 participants were asked how they experienced giving redirecting feedback. It was found that 44 per cent indicated that they experienced giving redirecting feedback as stressful and difficult, while 21 per cent said that they actually avoided giving feedback entirely. In addition, many leaders mistakenly assume that, while redirecting feedback should always be given, reinforcing feedback is merely optional. However, Zenger and Folkman's research shows that employees actually find it very important to receive reinforcing feedback, as such feedback positively links back to the employee themselves; by receiving positive feedback the employee feels as if they have been noticed by their leader, and that furthermore their contribution is appreciated. Giving reinforcing feedback ensures that your employees trust you and, as a result, these employees will also be more likely to receive critical or redirecting feedback in a more positive manner. A total of 72 per cent of employees that took part in the aforementioned survey indicated that their performance would improve if their managers would provide more redirecting feedback.[86]

It is important to understand that our feedback can be both redirecting and reinforcing, with various sources referring to an ideal ratio of 1:4 or 1:5. This means that, following a good redirecting feedback conversation, it will be necessary hold four or five reinforcing feedback conversations. This is in order to continue properly indicating appreciation for the worker's activities as well as to maintain trust in one another.

Try to remain clear regarding the purpose of the reinforcing feedback conversation in question. The so-called sandwich approach – in which you start positively, then send out a negative message, then end on a positive note – creates confusion and can lead to incorrect interpretations. When asked about such sandwich conversations, people tend to indicate either 'Well, it was not too bad, I only hear the good news anyway', or 'It was difficult because, in the end, I only heard something negative'. 'What does the feedback giver actually want from me?' and 'Is what I hear now actually genuine?' are questions that come into the mind of the feedback receiver after using the sandwich approach.

A leader's ability to provide useful feedback has a significant effect on employee engagement. Such a relationship was demonstrated in a study by Zenger and Folkman conducted among more than 22,000 leaders.[87] Leaders who scored high on providing honest feedback received a very high rating from their employees when it came to employee engagement (scoring at the 77th percentile). In contrast, those leaders who gave little to no honest feedback according to the employee responses, scored at the 25th percentile in regard to employee engagement (see Figure 6.6 for the graphical representation). It is therefore clear that employees want to receive honest feedback from their leaders.

But how do you give reinforcing and redirecting feedback in the right way – that is, in a way that keeps emotional responses on the right track? Let us start with the kind of feedback that has the greatest effect: reinforcing feedback.

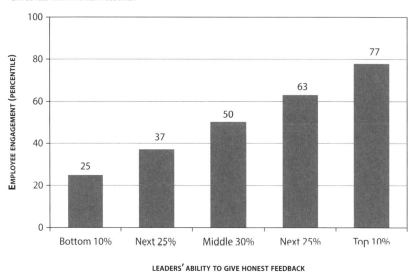

Figure 6.6: Employees want honest feedback. (Source: *Harvard Business Review*, Zenger & Folkman, 2013)

Reinforcing feedback

Reinforcing feedback: Motivational feedback that recognizes those attitudes and behaviours that have contributed effectively to a goal.

This means that you consciously observe employees to show them that you notice them, and that you recognize their contributions to the organization and team goals. This sends out a positive signal, and you therefore meet the needs of every person in regard to them having meaning in their life and in their work – their need belong somewhere, and their need to be involved in what they do. You are careful and diligent, but also 'to the point' when providing reinforcing feedback. This can also take place in workplace corridors, without needing to 'sit someone down', and does not even have to take up much time. When following the steps indicated here, this process can be completed within one or two minutes (see box).

Giving reinforcing feedback
– Identify and describe the behaviours or traits you want to stimulate.
– State the impact this has on you, the team, and the entire organization.
– Show your personal appreciation.

Why is it important that you emphasise the effect of the behaviour or trait? If you apply this mode of reinforcing feedback, you will find that it ensures that:

a.   The feedback is more specific.
b.   The recipient also sees the effect of what they have done (or what they are doing) in regard to team goals, and that their behaviour has clear consequences.
c.   It becomes visible that you, as a feedback giver, are attentive to the contributions the feedback recipient makes in regard to the team.

The question may now arise in your mind as to how often you should express your appreciation when providing reinforcing feedback:

d.   Once per conversation is enough. This makes the conversation personal rather than distant, and it ensures an improved emotional and personal connection with the feedback giver.

As an example, I give the school leader who walks through their school's corridors several times each day, and who and observes the behaviour of teachers and their interactions with their students. These observations allow the school leader to have short reinforcing feedback conversations with the teacher, so that the teacher better understands which behaviour positively impacts the students, thereby achieving those objectives set by the school and their team. In addition, the teacher feels that their daily interactions with the students are recognized. This gives the teacher an enormous boost to continue with their profession: improving the learning of their students.

Redirecting feedback

As mentioned before when discussing reinforcing feedback, it is also important to give targeted redirecting feedback. We do not have to organize a redirecting feedback session or discussion for everything and anything that fails to meet our highest expectations. However, when patterns that threaten the achievement of our objectives do arise, we must engage in a redirecting feedback session or discussion. However, we must do this in a careful and cautious manner.

Redirecting Feedback: Feedback that enables the feedback recipient to correct their behaviour or develop their competencies and motivation.

This definition indicates that through redirecting feedback – while also paying attention to our human emotions – we are able to adjust behaviour. Considering everything that has been said about providing redirecting feedback thus far, it is clearly a challenge to do so in a positive way. Fortunately, Kathleen Stinnett's work provides us with the tools we need to help us give redirecting feedback. In the book *The Extraordinary Coach*, which she co-wrote with John Zenger, Stinnett provides a particularly useful model (the FUEL model) for ensuring that redirecting feedback discussions run in an effective and reinforcing way.[88] While this model is by no means intended to provide a rigid plan or schematic that should be followed to the letter, it nevertheless offers us the purchase by which we can deal with difficult and different situations, and helps us ensure that any emotional reactions that might arise are dealt with properly and accordingly.

FUEL is an abbreviation of the four steps that are to be taken during a redirecting feedback conversation, and ensures that you can keep the conversation going.

–	Frame	Frame the conversation.
–	Understand	Understand the Current State.
–	Explore	Explore the desired situation.
–	Lay out	Layout a successful plan.

The acronym FUEL describes exactly what we are looking for in this situation: the fuel to start and keep redirecting feedback conversations going. A point-by-point discussion of each step is provided in the box below.

The FUEL model

FRAME – frame the conversation
This means that the feedback giver clarifies the goal and the desired conversational outcome so that both parties can arrive at a number of improvement actions together.
Make sure the setting implies that the conversation is serious and treat the recipient with respect. During the first step of the conversation you might, for example, say:
- *I would like to talk with you about (behaviour, performance, situation), is this a good time?*
- *I would like to share some observations with you and hear your views on them.*
- *At the end of this conversation I would like… (desired outcome).*

UNDERSTAND – gain insight into the current situation
During this part of the conversation, both the feedback giver and the feedback receiver want to understand what is going on and what its effect will be on the organization/team. When done properly, the understanding and awareness of both the giver and the receiver will increase.
– *Can I share some observations with you? (Give one or two examples of events/ behaviours.)*
– *What do you think is happening here? How do you see this situation?*
– *What does this mean for you? What does this mean for others in the team? What does this mean for your results?*
– *What are the consequences if you do not change this behaviour?*

EXPLORE – explore the desired situation
The feedback giver explores several alternatives and possibilities for improvement with the recipient. As a giver you can also name or clarify perspective in regard to the redirecting conversation.
– *Let us talk about the desired situation from both our perspectives; accordingly, what does the situation look like according to your perspective?*
– *What steps could you take to achieve this? What works for you in this context?*
– *May I make a suggestion?*
– *What do you think might be your biggest challenge in achieving this desired outcome?*

LAY OUT – design a plan of action
The feedback giver supports the receiver in formulating steps for improvement. Together you identify specific and concrete objectives and actions for improvement.
– *What specific and concrete steps are you going to take? Between now and when can I expect to see that you have… (desired outcome)?*
– *How can I help you with this? Who else could support you?*
– *Let's continue this conversation (set date and time).*

When holding a conversation in accordance with the steps presented in FUEL you make sure that the recipient has the 'space' they need to present and discuss their perspective. Furthermore, you treat the feedback receiver with respect and ensure that concrete and specific agreements are made concerning those actions they need to take. The goal here is to motivate the feedback receiver to change their behaviour, particularly by inviting them to come up with ideas on how to do this. Offer guidance where and when it is necessary. The eight human emotions and needs discussed earlier in this

chapter are respected so that you can maintain control over the message
you intend to send.

The FUEL model differs from the commonly used DESC feedback model.
I mention the DESC model explicitly because many professionals know
this model well and try to apply it when providing redirecting feedback.
I will now give an example of the application of this model as it is often
carried out.

1. **D**escribe the perceived behaviour: *I have noticed that you spend a lot of time each day reviewing and checking the work activities of our team.*
2. **E**xpress how this behaviour affects you: *This gives me the feeling that you do not trust your colleagues/us.*
3. **S**pecify what you would like them to do differently: *I would therefore ask you not to do this again.*
4. **S**hare the Consequences of their behaviour change: *This way we feel less controlled, which helps us be more open to taking the initiative within the team.*

However good the intention may be regarding the identification of – as
well as the striving to improve or change – this unwanted behaviour, the
disadvantage of the DESC model is that it does not encourage us to actively
inquire into the intentions and perspective of the other; therefore, it prevents
us from finding the possible causes of the other person's behaviour. The result
is that, when expressing your feelings, the other person might quickly come
to the conclusion that you do not understand them, or that your feelings
are not interesting to them. Continuing the conversation would therefore
have no value.

We must be careful not to reason only according to our own perspective
and in doing so climb the ladder of inference too quickly. Our ideas are
based on our own experiences. Accordingly, the perspective of the other
is necessary in order to reach a mutual understanding and, from such
an understanding, proceed good actions. This poses a challenge for both
parties, however, without this process feedback will be useless in facilitating
improvement and connection between these individuals. After all, feedback
is about feeding information to one another for common improvement.

*Summary: Feedback is a process whereby we openly consider our behaviour
in relation to what we want to achieve through this behaviour. Good intentions
are only visible to others through our behaviour. By talking to one another
and inviting one another to take a look at our behaviour with the objective of
improving ourselves, we can continue to learn from each another. To achieve*

this aim we need both reinforcing feedback (i.e. am I doing the right things and what contributions do they make in regard to what we want to achieve?) and, where necessary, redirecting feedback (so that we can notice and identify patterns in our behaviour that might actually jeopardize the achievement of our goal). Feedback is always based on a positive intention: the power to keep learning from each other.

That we can learn from one another certainly becomes visible when we try to hand over the baton to a new generation. Over the years, different generations have developed their own way of seeing and acting. In the next chapter, we take a look at the different perspectives of these generations and indicate what these different perspectives mean for leadership.

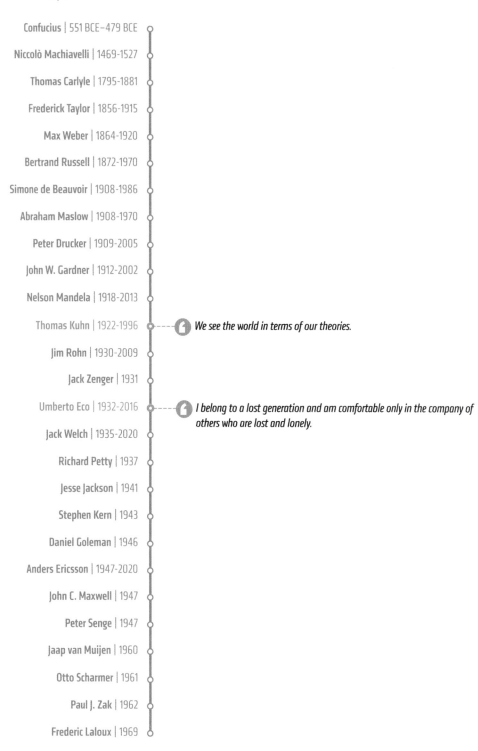

Confucius | 551 BCE–479 BCE

Niccolò Machiavelli | 1469-1527

Thomas Carlyle | 1795-1881

Frederick Taylor | 1856-1915

Max Weber | 1864-1920

Bertrand Russell | 1872-1970

Simone de Beauvoir | 1908-1986

Abraham Maslow | 1908-1970

Peter Drucker | 1909-2005

John W. Gardner | 1912-2002

Nelson Mandela | 1918-2013

Thomas Kuhn | 1922-1996   *We see the world in terms of our theories.*

Jim Rohn | 1930-2009

Jack Zenger | 1931

Umberto Eco | 1932-2016   *I belong to a lost generation and am comfortable only in the company of others who are lost and lonely.*

Jack Welch | 1935-2020

Richard Petty | 1937

Jesse Jackson | 1941

Stephen Kern | 1943

Daniel Goleman | 1946

Anders Ericsson | 1947-2020

John C. Maxwell | 1947

Peter Senge | 1947

Jaap van Muijen | 1960

Otto Scharmer | 1961

Paul J. Zak | 1962

Frederic Laloux | 1969

7.   Leadership through the generations

I belong to a lost generation and am comfortable only in the company
of others who are lost and lonely.
– Umberto Eco (1932–2016), Italian writer

Seeing, sensing, and managing a generation-aware organization and society has always been an important theme. Generation Y is currently striving to be heard more and more in regard to the political plans of various parties. So, are these parties aware of the impact their policy proposals will have on the generation that is just starting to enter the labour market in earnest? An age difference of just 5–10 years, for instance, can make the difference between merely visualizing a new development and actually feeling the consequences of that development. A good example of this is the debate about possible changes to the pension system.

The solution to being able to properly deal with the speed and unpredictability of societal developments – as well as, more specifically, the effects of these on our labour market – is generation management, which also involves having an eye for the effect of these developments according to each generation. If organizations adopt a more inclusive policy, then this should lead to optimal cooperation between the generations; in turn, this will help to cope with the pace and pressure within the labour market generated by the inflow of new employees and the outflow of older workers.

The Generation Pact, which has now been developed within various sectors of the labour market in the Netherlands, is a good example of cooperation between the generations. The Generation Pact allows older employees to work fewer hours without sacrificing a directly proportional share of their salary. The so-called '60–80–100 division' that results from this Pact is an elaboration of commitment and reward. An employee will work for 60 per cent of their current working hours, but will be paid 80 per cent of their income while still keeping 100 per cent of their pension accrual. This system ensures that older employees who are reaching their physical and mental limits – for example, those working in the healthcare or construction sectors – can continue to do their work with more energy and a lower dropout rate. At the same time, members of younger

generations are given the opportunity to move up faster within their organizations, partly because of the release of budget this system provides.

Generation management

Generation management is a term that is now being embraced by large
companies. Comparatively, generational thinking is a term that has been
used for much longer in order to explain human behaviour through the ages.
Laloux's work is a good example of this. Laloux has been able to interpret,
divide, and categorize people's actions and the various zeitgeists of the past
100 years into different eras, and has even classified interpreted the time
before this into larger cohorts of 1000 years each.[89]

There has always been considerable ambiguity concerning the meaning
of the word 'generation'. Broadly speaking, generation refers to a group of
individuals who were *born roughly around the same year of life*, and *who have
experienced the same societal events and changes*. The origin of the word
'generation' can be found in ancient Greek; γένος (genos) can be literally
translated as 'origin', 'birth', and 'descent'. This allows us to interpret the
meaning of the term with even greater precision. Individuals from the same
generation have at least lived through and have encountered the same reality
and prevailing societal ideas.

The history of generation theory began many years ago and cannot
be defined according to a one-sided approach. The difference between
a synchronous and a diachronic approach already yields two completely
opposite interpretations of the concept.

–   The diachronic approach to generation strongly emphasizes continuity.
    For example, when speaking about the first, second, and third gene-
    ration of immigrants and newcomers in a country, this can be seen as
    a diachronic approach to the concept. A newly born son or daughter
    is seen as a new generation relative to their parents. This makes this
    approach a very consistent and continuous means of classification
    whereby, according to this approach, generation theory has in fact
    already started with the birth of the first human.
–   Comparatively, a synchronous approach describes a generation more
    in terms of one's generational peers. Radical events, an unbalanced
    economy, or other large-scale historical events result in a certain *esprit
    de corps* among generational peers. Accordingly, a large part of oneself is
    recognized in others because both have lived through the same events
    and experiences. Although everyone will deal with these events and

experiences in their own particular way, the consistently repeated ideas and ideologies of leaders and parties in power within society generate a strong bond among people. This marks a so-called zeitgeist, or 'mainstream spirit' of the time. Responses to this zeitgeist can therefore often be found in a certain resisting, rebellious, or opposing behaviour.

One example that had a significant effect on Dutch society can be seen in the so-called *nozems* of the 1950s. At the time these individuals were described, in a somewhat trivializing manner, as comprising a riotous youth culture. However, the philosophy of the *nozems* themselves paints a picture of far greater depth and nuance: 'Down with the values of yesterday. There is no point, everything is a coincidence'. This morality propounded by the *nozems*, rather than being a riotous youth culture, presents a somewhat disillusioned and distrustful image of society. Not only in the Netherlands, but also globally, was this development clearly visible among young people at the time and was not overlooked in society: in the US they spoke of 'greasers'; in France, the 'blousons noirs'; in Germany, the 'Halbstarken'; and in England, 'Teddy boys'.

If we look a decade further on, to the 60s, we can again identify a group of provocative young people among contemporary trendsetters. The *provos* fought for a new ideal due to their dissatisfaction with the prevailing ideology at the time. According to the *provos*, man had lost himself amid the booming economy that followed the Second World War. Through many playful actions and brutal but peaceful demonstrations and occupations, this group of young people tried to attract attention to their cause and, through a certain solidarity, rebelled against what they thought was a lack of idealism in their time.

When we compare the slogans of these rebellious youth groups – the *nozems* and the *provos* – the synchronous division of the generation theory seems appropriate and quite correct. While it is true that we can observe that these peers differed in regard to their direction, depth, and priorities, the ideology and views that were anchored in society at that time nevertheless remained a common good. The interweaving of generation theory with historical sciences has actually caused the start of a new field of study: Generation management.

> *Generation management is a specifically developed form of life-phase aware staff and personnel policy. It is based on the principle that all employees of all ages make a valuable contribution, each in their own particular way.*[90]

Based on a synchronous division of generations, the Dutch sociologist and historian Van Doorn made a striking distinction between 'fellow fighters' and 'fellow sufferers' within generations.[91] These fellow fighters are associated with especially active generations, those that act decisively as a result of shocking events and profound changes, and whose presence is prominent in their particular era. Fellow fighters are often written about in the history books because a lot was going on in their time, there was action and these fellow fighters had a clear public face and voice. Comparatively, there are 'fellow sufferers' who are, perhaps, a bit like the neglected children. These individuals are generational peers who reluctantly accept their fate. While these individuals do want to fight, they do not see the point of doing so in an attention-seeking manner, and aim to fight without 'bells and whistles'. It is possible that these groups may even lack specific ideals. Fellow sufferers are often people who have endured such a traumatic experience that merely sitting out any further developments is enough for them. My own generation – the so-called 'lost generation' (this term was coined by sociologist Henk Becker in his 1997 book, *Toekomst van de verloren generatie* ('The Future of the Lost Generation') – offers a good example of the latter. This generation saw many people remain consciously unemployed: 'If there are no jobs available for me, don't expect me to fight for them myself'. After 35 years we still see such generational peers consciously sticking to this behaviour, individuals who might still not have a formally registered job.

Such a historical and synchronous approach to generations is in line with Becker's definition of a *generation*:[92]

> Generation: 'A category of coevals whose behaviour shows the effects of one or a few unique contemporary changes that these individuals experienced during their formative years.'

It is precisely these formative years that are so important because they concern the period between the ages of 10–25 years. These are the years in which people create an identity, shape their norms and values, and develop their expectations. Severe discontinuous changes during this stage of life cause transitions within certain eras and form the basis for generational changes. Examples of such profound and discontinuous changes include the Second World War, deep economic recessions, the rise of the Internet, natural disasters, and – that which we face today – pandemics. It will be interesting to see the impact of our current zeitgeist around the COVID-19 pandemic on today's young generation.

Interest in generations is not a trend that is unique to our current time. Philosopher of science Thomas Kuhn put forward the concept of paradigm shift as early as 1922. He argued that the way in which a group of contemporaries interpret specific events, how an era is experienced, how this group of contemporaries experience that era, and how they view society all depend on the prevailing contemporary paradigm. Accordingly, the views and ideas of the paradigm itself, as it were, frame the view of its contemporaries. Peers are therefore dependent on the paradigm in which they live, while also being restricted by its limitations. According to Kuhn, it is not a matter of experiencing the world as it really is, but rather a matter of how the world is experienced within a certain period.

The structure of society has always heavily depended on science and its factual representation of reality. Only after sufficient factual and rational evidence has been gathered to irrevocably undermine the current paradigm, will the old paradigm be exchanged for a new one.

We see the world in terms of our theories.
– Thomas Kuhn (1922–1996) American scientist, philosopher, and historian

The classic example of a paradigm shift is, of course, Galileo Galilei's discovery of the heliocentric model and the corresponding worldview. Accordingly, the previous outdated theory had to make way for rock-solid new evidence: that the Earth does not occupy a central place in the universe.

Paradigm shifts are not only observable within science; they can also take place on a smaller scale, such as within a human life. At some point, everyone experiences something so novel that it forces out the old way of doing things in order to make room for the new. The fact that COVID-19 has made us look differently at the effects of nitrogen, noise, and congestion in cities and on motorways gives us a powerful impulse to really innovate in the relevant sectors. The new simply cannot coexist with the old, and it is at times like these that people change their thoughts and ideas. A person's formative years – in which impressions and experiences are the most influential – will in that sense also be the period in which they are most sensitive to such paradigm shifts. However, there is no specific time frame within which a paradigm shift should occur. Indeed, the term *paradigm* allows for no continuity; rather, it is strongly dependent on the speed at which humanity develops.

Generational effects in the workplace

Generations, on the other hand, are subject to a certain period since human life is time-bound. Differences in age and the ever-changing zeitgeist within which employees grew up form an unavoidable point of attention for organizations. Never before has the labour market known such a wide range of generationally oriented expectations, norms and values, and ideals and needs among its employees. Major challenges lie ahead for our society due to the mass retirement of the oldest generation and the fact that fewer and fewer children are being born in the Western world. Young people entering the labour market are becoming increasingly scarce. The hunt for so-called 'talent' will require an increasing number of sectors to devise new recruitment ideas, methods, and means of binding and captivating this young generation. Not only young people will be sorely needed in facing the societal challenges ahead, but also those generations that are set to take over directly over from the oldest generation: Generation X and, now increasingly so, Generation Y (see Figure 7.1). Retaining employees from these generations will be equally important as recruiting new people with potential. Actions within the framework of a targeted generation management policy are characterized by responding to the needs, wishes, and motivations of each generation – in the article 'Het Démasqué van de Generatiekloof' ('The Unmasking of the Generation Gap') these actions are explained according to each generation.[93] In addition to paying attention to personal goals, utilization of knowledge and skills will also optimize organizations: forming and sharing views, values, and practices leads to an optimal execution and organization of work actions.[94]

According to Aart Bontekoning, the picture is only really complete when both approaches – organizational culture and generation theory – are brought together. Generations can be seen as subcultural layers that function within organizations, whereby the top layer represents the oldest generation, and the bottom layer represents the youngest generation. While the top layer may have a major effect on the organization it is, despite its advanced age and experience, likely also to be a relatively small group. As the oldest generation slowly disappears, so too does their influence on organizational cultures. A new generation will now take over the top layer and bring with it a different influence style. If it is our challenge to devise and create new forms of cooperation and coexistence, we must do so by including all generations.

With the outflow of the oldest generation and the influx of younger generations, we can therefore speak of a generational shift. The consequences of this are especially noticeable regarding the values of an organization. The cultures of many organizations are undergoing rejuvenation, and their system of norms and values is undergoing a transition. After all, defining and directing an organizational culture begins with higher management formulating its own norms and values. A new generation being at the top layer of an organization can break old patterns, add new elements, and apply contemporary strategies to determine the direction of that organization. This can provide the organization with a very welcome breath of fresh air and considerable vitality. On the other hand, new generations at the top still too often get stuck in fixed patterns of prevailing organizational cultures, while the major benefits of joining the various generational forces in question remains regularly underutilized.

Generational changes are noticeable, not only in the workplace, but within all of in society. The rejuvenation in politics provides new possibilities and opportunities to enable and make such transitions possible. We do not only see this rejuvenation taking place in the Netherlands, but also in Finland, France, Canada, Denmark, and New Zealand.

Four generations

Currently, four different generations are active in the workplace: decreasing numbers of baby boomers; Generation X, the largest group in the workplace; the new and emerging group of organizational leaders, Generation Y/millennials; and, finally, the youngest group of new entrants to the labour market, Generation Z. Who are these people and how do these generations differ from one another? Figure 7.1 shows a number of keywords that apply to generations in the workplace, after which a more detailed description is provided of the contexts in which these generations grew up.

Baby boomers 1945–1960	Generation X 1961–1980	Generation Y/ millennials 1981–1995	Generation Z 1995–2010
Freedom	Experience	Passion	Meaning
Consensus	Balance	Diversity	Equality
Ideal	Sceptical	Discovering	Activism
Loyal	Bridge builders	Entrepreneurs	Sustainable
(Re)structuring	Professionalizing	Organizing yourself	Constantly improving
Participation	Adjusting	Achieving	Results

Figure 7.1: Four generations in the workplace; characteristics per generation according to the (international) cohort classification.

Baby boomers (year of birth: 1945–1960)

This generation grew up in Western Europe during a period of post-war economic growth. During the post-war period of reconstruction and rebuilding, it was easy for these individuals to find a job after they had completed their education and training. During their early years, the so-called hippie movement was in full swing along with, in the Netherlands, the process of 'de-pillarization' and secularization. There was also a concurrent sexual revolution, and contraception allowed this generation to decide for themselves how many children to have and when to have them. The baby boom generation is also referred to as the 'protest generation'.

> *Hippie culture was a subculture among young people in the second half of the 1960s. As a youth and counterculture, this subculture was popular among teenagers and those in their twenties. Hippies are seen as the 'makers' of the flower-power movement and are therefore associated with the sexual, musical, and social revolution(s) of the 1960s and 1970s. (Source: Wikipedia)*

Terms that fit the zeitgeist of this generation include 'cultural revolution', 'prosperous economy', 'urbanization and industrialization', 'waves of immigration', and 'children of prosperity'. Highlighting the many opportunities of growth and accrued rights for this generation is a theme that is often still found in the media. Problems related to, for example, pensions and the continuing commitment of employees will keep our attention for the time being. This is perhaps the most talked about generation so far, and it is one against which the younger generation in particular is rebelling with increasing fervour.

Generation X (year of birth: 1961–1980)

In the Netherlands this age group (as described above) was called 'the lost generation' by Henk Becker. It was later referred to in the media and internationally as 'Generation X' and 'Generation nix'. This is not a particularly positive name for a generation who grew up in a less flourishing time than their predecessors. A characteristic of this generation was high youth unemployment, and hence the name 'lost' was soon coined. Many highly educated young people from this generation were unable to find a job. However, this generation generally preferred not to express itself through protest, and chose instead to express itself through music, as lovers of punk, disco, or soul. The parents of this generation (who mostly belonged to the 'silent generation') gave their children a lot of space and freedom throughout their upbringing. One characteristic people from Generation X share is a no-nonsense attitude. This generation also tried out and sampled new forms of cohabitation, an example of which can be seen in the so-called LAT relationships (i.e. couples living apart together) and in people living together who have children but who are not married. In fact, Generation X is the generation with the fewest formal marriages. If we can characterize the zeitgeist of this generation it would include the polarized and conflicted decade of the 1970s, crisis in the 1980s, as well as unemployment, mergers/acquisitions, and failing institutions.

Generation Y/millennials (year of birth: 1981–1995)

After Generation X, a new generation arrived and with it came a new era of prosperity. As the millennium approached, the people born during these years were referred to as millennials. The zeitgeist of this time is characterized by economic prosperity and technological progress, with the large organizations of the time trying to entice this generation to join them *en masse*.

Most millennials are children of the baby boom generation. Born in a time of prosperity and economic growth, these children were allowed to have a say in and make decisions about everything in their upbringing. Due to the relatively smaller families (following a shift from quantity to quality) of the time, these children received a lot of attention, and many were raised in an easy-going manner. This has made the millennials a spoiled generation in the eyes of the older generations.

> *The term 'French fries generation' (applicable to children born between 1970 and 1985) is the name of a sub-generation that was given a separate status in the Netherlands by trainers such Leo Beenhakker (a Dutch international football coach), who used the term to describe, in his eyes, spoiled and easy-going young athletes.*

In addition, this generation grew up in a time when it was thought that everything could be made. Expectations were therefore high! This is the first time that burnout and pressure to perform started to appear at a young age. Conversely, the generation itself places many demands on employers. Terms that characterize this generation include *information technology, globalization, making demands*, and *anything is possible*.

Generation Z (year of birth: 1995–2010)

This was the first generation that were born into an already existing digital world. Accordingly, for this generation there is no life without the Internet. The term we often use for people of this generation is 'digital natives'; these individuals were not born into an era defined by growth and manufacturability, but rather an uncertain world with the threat of terrorism and financial crises. The aftermath of the traumatic 9/11 attacks (the events of 11 September in 2001) is huge for this generation.

This generation was raised by Generation X, and so their parents were more down to earth compared with baby boomers. As a result, this Generation is viewed in a different way. It is important for people from Generation Z to have a good understanding of what is going on in the world. We see a big difference here from the way in which Generation Y was raised. The older generations, the X and baby boom generations, experience Generation Z as being more realistic and conservative than Generation Y. An important characteristic of Generation Z is that they are open to ethnic, cultural, and sexual diversity and freedom. The financial crisis, the threat of terrorism, the digital world, environmental awareness, and awareness of a world of equality and inequality are concepts that exemplify this generation.

Leadership and generations

When looking at the different characteristics of the generations, it is also interesting to see whether these generations show different nuances and emphases in terms of their leadership. Is the impact of their upbringing and its concurrent zeitgeist also visible in the way in which they have developed and the way in which they show their own leadership? If we rely on the nuances and emphasis discussed, which are also described in various media and by contemporary generation experts, we see a shift in leadership from *ego* to *eco*. Where the leadership style of baby boomers is still very much carried out according to their position or role – and the power that goes with it – we can slowly but surely see that the working environment, and the impact on the environment, become increasingly important over time. These is a decreased emphasis on the formal position (the ego), and more on how you – both as a person in your environment, as well as actively with your environment – can make a contribution (the ecosystem). Accordingly there is an ongoing development of risk-averse behaviour with regard to meeting challenges together in order to grow as

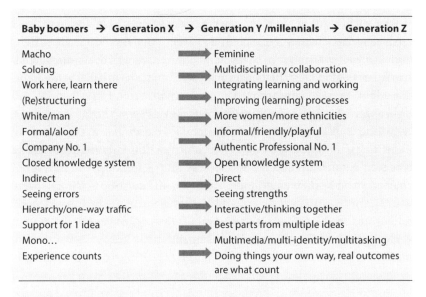

Baby boomers → Generation X → Generation Y /millennials → Generation Z	
Macho	Feminine
Soloing	Multidisciplinary collaboration
Work here, learn there	Integrating learning and working
(Re)structuring	Improving (learning) processes
White/man	More women/more ethnicities
Formal/aloof	Informal/friendly/playful
Company No. 1	Authentic Professional No. 1
Closed knowledge system	Open knowledge system
Indirect	Direct
Seeing errors	Seeing strengths
Hierarchy/one-way traffic	Interactive/thinking together
Support for 1 idea	Best parts from multiple ideas
Mono…	Multimedia/multi-identity/multitasking
Experience counts	Doing things your own way, real outcomes are what count

Figure 7.2: The older we get, the more open we are to feedback. (Source: *Harvard Business Review*, Zenger & Folkman, 2016)

a whole, and a development from a mono- (one-sided) to a multicultural (multi-sided and plural) approach.

Multiculturalism is given greater emphasis in society, with concrete international examples of this being seen in leaders such as Barack Obama and Nelson Mandela. The theme of contemporary leadership concerns the shift from diversity to inclusion (see also Chapter 9). In the table below, this shift is illustrated in terms of characteristics.

But how is this reflected in the data concerning leaders from these different generations? And can we also see that the shift of leadership as described herein (i.e. from ego to eco) creates a different dynamic within organizations? A 2018 study by Academica, conducted among more than 1,150 education leaders and described in the article *De staat van de Nederlandse onderwijsleider*, shows a number of interesting developments.[95]

Generation Y/millennials have a higher average leadership score (according to their 360-degree feedback scores obtained from their professional colleagues, their managers and leaders, and the employees they supervise) compared with the other generations. Comparatively, the baby boom generation scores the lowest on average. It is remarkable that Generation Y scores high on behaviours that concern integrity and honesty, taking initiative, result-orientation, powerful communication, being prolifically, and encouraging others to develop themselves.

One might think this higher leadership score would have a positive effect on the engagement scores of employees of these Generation Y leaders. Here, however, we see an interesting phenomenon: on average, these engagement scores turn out to be no higher, on average, than those of other generations of leaders. This deviates from the (inter)national trend that leaders with higher scores for their leadership competencies also score higher, on average, regarding employee engagement. If we take a closer look at this cohort of millennials, we can see enormous differences within this group; this alone is reason enough to take a closer look at this generation, which is often characterized by their environment as being difficult and less predictable.

A closer look at Generation Y/millennials

The challenge for our generation is to create a world where everyone has a sense of purpose.
– Mark Zuckerberg (1984), American computer programmer, entrepreneur, and co-founder of Facebook

In 2005, Steve Jobs (a member of the baby boomer generation) gave a speech to Stanford University graduates. In the speech he talked about the necessity of finding passion in your work and in your life. Twelve years later, Mark Zuckerberg (a member of the millennial generation) gives the element of passion a new dimension with his declaration, 'The challenge for our generation is to create a world where everyone has a sense of purpose.'

Fascination concerning Generation Y is considerable at the moment. Articles often describe why this group is so different from previous generations. Generation Y is the first generation in history to have grown up in a world of digital technology, and these articles extensively describe certain characteristics that 'exclusively' belong to Generation Y and how millennials should be treated. As described briefly above, this generation is one of high expectations.

Common views about Generation Y are that it needs flexibility, is addicted to positive feedback because of its 'like' culture, and is easily bored and self-absorbed. In a study conducted within various sectors in the Netherlands, CBE Group, on the other hand, describes this generation as one that pursues **challenge**, **meaning**, and **connection**, with core factors such as development, enthusiasm, and fun.[96]

Meanwhile, this generation comprises over 43 per cent of the working world. Interestingly, this group is often perceived as being one of 'difficult' employees. A member of Generation Y is often the new young leader in the workplace between the baby boomers and Xers; after these millennials, the young Generation Z is just making its entrance.

The question that is often asked is: 'How can organizations deal with this generation, which has been labelled as "difficult" in the eyes of the other generations?' As a leader it is important that you have knowledge of the social influences on various generations, but that you also remain vigilant against negative stereotypes. Focusing on this generation is undertaken with the intention of exploring discussions and patterns that we often see in the workplace, as well as to offer executives some purchase in regard to these discussions and patterns.

An important phenomenon among Generation Y is the increased pressure to perform. More than half of this group has been provided with scientific training or education and therefore they have many options from which to choose; however, this also has a downside.

Research by ArboNed shows that an estimated 100,000 of the 1.3 million millennials in the Netherlands are at home with burnout symptoms.[97]

When you deny generational differences you also deny the related problems, says Jasper Scholten, a millennial.[98] According to Scholten, millennials have high expectations, which leads to great insecurity within this group. Janka Stoker, professor of leadership and organizational change, however, doubts whether this uncertainty is characteristic of the millennial generational group.[99] She argues that stage of life is a more important factor in determining how confident or insecure someone feels. An employee over 50 years of age simply has more experience and is, as a result of this, more certain of their capabilities. A study conducted by Zenger and Folkman confirms Stoker's view: with age, self-confidence grows, and with it, a greater sense of comfort when receiving feedback (see Figure 7.3).[100]

It can be seen self-awareness among both men and women grows as they become older; however, we can also see that this effect is even stronger among women. The challenge is to ask and to provide more feedback (see also Chapter 6) within and between all generational groups, and through this we can support the youngest generation in a positive way in regard to their development.

The question we need to ask ourselves is: What is the impact of feedback on this generation and how can we give millennials feedback so that they can better deal with the stress they experience when having to choose – and when dealing with – the dilemma of 'I want and can do anything?'

The Older We Get, the More We're Open to Self-Improvement

Percentile of people who identify with an "improving" mindset

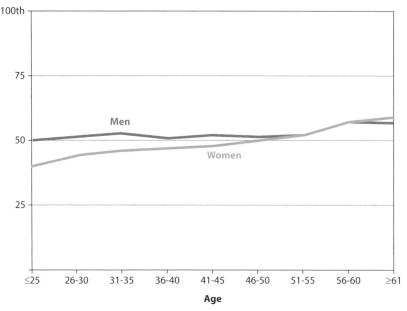

Figure 7.3: The older we get, the more open we are to feedback. (Source: *Harvard Business Review*, Zenger & Folkman, 2016)

What feedback does Generation Y want?

It is remarkable that many people who write about Generation Y do not belong to this generation. For this reason, researchers Zenger and Folkman decided to let Generation Y themselves have a say; they investigated what kind of feedback this generation would like to receive in order to optimize employee performance as well as the approach of leaders.

One of the questions from their questionnaire was:
If I had my choice, I would prefer to receive:
– Praise or recognition for a job well done.
Or
– Some helpful, redirecting feedback.

A total of 66 per cent indicated that they preferred to receive helpful and redirecting feedback (see Figure 7.4). This need for useful and redirecting feedback was stronger in Generation Y than in any other generational group. This finding is contrary to popular belief.

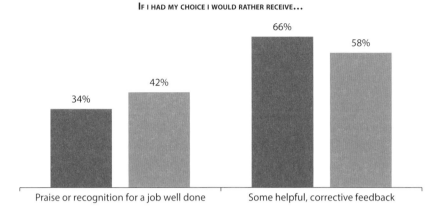

Figure 7.4: Generation Y wants helpful, redirecting feedback. (Source: Forbes, 2014)

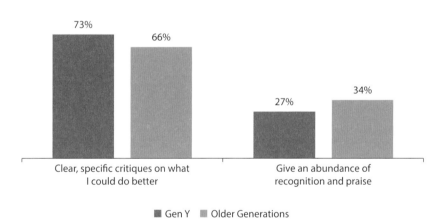

Figure 7.5: Generation Y wants clear and specific critiques on what they could do better. (Source: Forbes, 2014)

To further substantiate this effect, the following statement was tested: *What I appreciate most from my manager is...*

– Clear, specific critiques as to what I could do better

Or

– An abundance of recognition and praise

Overall, 73 per cent of Generation Y indicated that they wanted clear and specific criticism, while after further questioning, a remarkable 80 per cent indicated that redirecting feedback would make them stronger regarding their performance (see Figure 7.5).

Now the following question remains: how does Generation Y deal with this feedback? Wanting to receive redirecting feedback is not the same as being able to properly deal with such feedback. We know from Zenger and Folkman's research that age is correlated with confidence and being comfortable with receiving feedback. Comparatively, Generation Y is very curious about how they are performing in the workplace, but they still find it difficult to receive feedback. However, this phenomenon is not unique to Generation Y and can be explained by the phase of life currently being experienced by millennials. Perhaps might also explain the relatively lower employee engagement scores of the employees of Generation Y leaders?

Engagement: extra attention for Generation Y?

Generation Y has many options to choose from. According to generation expert Talitha Muusse, a lifelong connection to work – as was seen and experienced by previous generations – is no longer applicable to those in this generation.[101] Members of Generation Y are less likely to commit to an employer, and even in times of economic uncertainty the thought that the 'grass may be greener' elsewhere still prevails. In the Netherlands, this phenomenon has been reinforced by a consistently favourable labour market over a long period, according to Muusse. Despite economic fluctuations, there is nevertheless a demand for young, well-qualified personnel. For this reason, it is important that organizations consider how to maintain employee engagement among members of this group; leaders play a crucial role this process due to their influence on employee engagement (see also Chapter 4).

The question we can ask ourselves here is: *Are the behaviours that the best leaders display when giving feedback also effective for Generation Y?*

Several studies show that the most effective leaders, focus on three things:
- They listen carefully.
- They provide feedback regularly.
- They provide more reinforcing than redirecting feedback.

The conclusion that can be drawn from this is that Generation Y wants more clear, honest, and redirective feedback. However, the style and the way by which such feedback is delivered is of great importance. In the same Zenger and Folkman study on generations that was discussed in the previous subsection, employees from Generation Y was asked to rate leaders according to several behaviours; it was found that several leadership behaviours correlated strongly with increased trust in the millennial's manager or leader. The behaviour of leaders that greatly increases the level of trust of employees from Generation Y is the *ability to listen carefully to the employee's views*. Millennials do not wish to be bombarded with unexpected and unsolicited feedback. As discussed above, *receiving feedback regularly reduces anxiety* and, when feedback is given consistently, this anxiety is notably less. Members of Generation Y indicate that they want to *receive redirecting feedback* because it has the potential to do more for them. However, this feedback should only be given if a relationship has already been developed through obtaining reinforcing feedback.

Golden rules do not exist. However, for anyone who hopes to transition to a workplace in which generations work together positively and effectively, and in which Generation Y has now taken a prominent position, I would like to conclude with the following six points for increasing mutual engagement.

Increasing engagement
- Provide recognition/confirmation of work carried out and the contribution this has made to the organization.
- Recognize and acknowledge the performance delivered by the individual.
- Try to see the other person's perspective regarding the area or subject about which they are asking for feedback.
- Give reinforcing feedback and make sure the other person can learn something from it.
- Ask the other person for suggestions about, or reactions to, the feedback provided.
- Provide support when creating a plan for improvement.

Summary: Each generation leaves its footprint on society, but we must be aware that certain views about a generation can lead to generalized thinking. Every employee deserves your attention and respect regarding their various differences. In your approach as a professional and as a leader you can take these generational differences into account, thereby creating understanding and helping you to find a way to work together sympathetically and compassionately.

Generations Y and Z are the youngest generations in the workforce, and are now in need of recognition and positive impulses. They challenge us to provide then with redirecting and honest feedback. They are most receptive when this is combined with listening, recognition, and assurance. The nature

*of the communication that Generation Y uses itself is both result-oriented and
one of action.*

As part of the shift from the monocultural to the multicultural, a trend
described and discussed in the current chapter, further focus on gender
is a theme that cannot be missed. So, what are the relevant developments
when thinking about gender, and what does this mean for leadership? The
following chapter compares and focuses on the male–female relationship.

Confucius | 551 BCE–479 BCE

Niccolò Machiavelli | 1469-1527

Thomas Carlyle | 1795-1881

Frederick Taylor | 1856-1915

Max Weber | 1864-1920

Bertrand Russell | 1872-1970

Simone de Beauvoir | 1908-1986 — *One is not born, but rather becomes, a woman.*

Abraham Maslow | 1908-1970

Peter Drucker | 1909-2005

John W. Gardner | 1912-2002

Nelson Mandela | 1918-2013

Thomas Kuhn | 1922-1996

Jim Rohn | 1930-2009

Jack Zenger | 1931

Umberto Eco | 1932-2016

Jack Welch | 1935-2020

Richard Petty | 1937 — *Confidence is the factor that turns thoughts into judgments about what we are capable of, and that then transforms those judgments into action.*

Jesse Jackson | 1941

Stephen Kern | 1943

Daniel Goleman | 1946

Anders Ericsson | 1947-2020

John C. Maxwell | 1947

Peter Senge | 1947

Jaap van Muijen | 1960

Otto Scharmer | 1961

Paul J. Zak | 1962

Frederic Laloux | 1969

8.   Leadership male/female

We still think of a powerful man as a born leader
and a powerful woman as an anomaly.
– Margaret Atwood (1939), American author and political activist

It is interesting that, in the same era in which we have declared gender equality, women remain underrepresented in leadership positions. This sensitive issue becoming increasingly prominent. The fact that relatively few women hold top positions in organizations raises questions as to why women have limited access to leadership roles and as well as those factors causing this to be the case. We might state or claim in our marketing communications that we would like to see greater representation of women in top organizational positions, but in reality, such representation still lags behind. Though we praise women who do reach the top, we also immediately give reasons as to why these individuals succeeded and others did not: specifically, because ostensibly they represent an exceptional kind of woman and are, perhaps, more masculine than feminine?! Before we take a look at the leadership styles of men and women, and determine whether there are any differences between the two, let us first list some facts. If we want to realize or enact a transition in our own leadership, it is first necessary to see what we can learn from both male and female leaders.

While there has been an increase in the number of women entering middle management positions, women remain very scarce at among the topmost leadership roles.[102] Indeed, just 18 per cent of the top 500 Fortune organizations are women , and only 27 of the top 500 Fortune organizations have a female CEO (see Figure 8.1). Men hold more than half of all top executive positions, and the prevailing trend within organizations is: the higher up in the hierarchy of the organization, the greater the inequality there will be.[103] This trend of inequality is often referred to as the *glass ceiling effect*, a metaphor that represents those invisible barriers that prevent women from advancing within organizational hierarchies.

The unconscious attribution of leadership competencies

It is by no means original to point out that stereotypes exist concerning those behaviours that are associated with female and male competencies. This phenomenon is also referred to as our *gender bias*, and concerns an

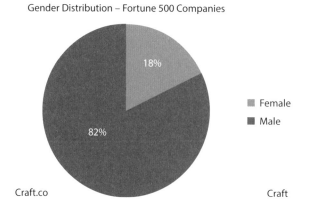

Figure 8.1: Male/female distribution in Fortune 500 companies. (Source: Craft Research, n.d.)

unconscious bias that has far-reaching consequences. Gender bias and gender stereotypes represent assumptions about the characteristics, behaviours, and role fulfilment of men and women. Research by Rudman and Glick shows that we are more likely to attribute behaviours such as being sensitive, warm, social, caring, and compassionate (*communal traits*) to women; comparatively, we are more likely to attribute characteristics such as ambition, assertiveness, competition, dominance, and independence (*agentic traits*) to men.[104] These latter qualities are precisely those qualities we associate with leadership, and such an association creates a role incongruity when a woman tries to take a leadership position. This is because stereotyped traits that are attributed to women are less likely to be associated with leadership behaviours.

For the majority of organizations, reconciling the stereotypical role attributed to women with a woman's potential to lead is a difficult process. Research shows that this gender bias results in women being considered as less effective in regard to them pursuing leadership positions, an effect that is enhanced if the woman in question is physically attractive or pregnant. While it is also true that this effect diminishes the longer a woman performs a leadership role, such implicit associations are, unfortunately, the most insidious – they can even affect our thinking without us realizing. Even a small bias can have far-reaching consequences. For example, a study conducted at Colombia University using computer simulations shows that a bias of just 1 per cent in favour of men can lead to an organizational culture in which only 35 per cent of all senior positions are filled by women.

People's preferences for certain types of leaders stems from, among other things, our evolutionary preferences, and the means by which individuals acquire power. The acquisition of power is based on a number of aspects, including a person's demographic and physical characteristics. To understand this, we must look far back into our evolutionary history and consider how leadership itself originated. Implicit leadership theories propound that we have leadership prototypes that we use to determine who we see as leaders. However, because these prototypes date from the time of our ancestors they are no longer appropriate or valid. This disparity leads to a so-called *evolutionary mismatch*: an evolutionary acquired trait or characteristic that was once beneficial or neutral, but that is no longer useful due to changes in our environment.

For example, in our ancestral environment it was beneficial for a leader to be physically fit and dominant. These qualities demonstrably increased the group's chances of survival during conflicts over scarce resources. During this period of our past, risks were mainly taken by men due to their greater physical fitness. As a result of these implicit evolutionary preferences, we consider how tall a leader is as being important when judging the effectiveness of their leadership. This is because we associate height with dominance, health, and intelligence. While the inclusion of superficial characteristics (such as height) when assessing effective leadership was a useful trait in our ancestral environment, it is no longer useful today. Despite this, a study conducted by the Vrije Universiteit Amsterdam and Oxford University shows that estimations concerning the effectiveness of a leader are still partially based on the leader's height: tall individuals are more likely to be seen as potential leaders. Furthermore, this effect is stronger in men than in it is in women.[105]

Napoleon complex

It is not without reason that, in his day, Napoleon was ridiculed for his height, as he was often depicted as being a small stocky man. Alfred Adler (1870–1937), a psychologist and psychiatrist, was the first person to use the term 'Napoleon complex'. According to Adler, Napoleon tried to compensate for his meagre height by displaying extremely ambitious behaviour. Today, the relationship between height and leadership remains a popular topic among various media. For example, former French president Nicolas Sarkozy (1955–) was ridiculed for his height for years. A Google search for Sarkozy's height yields several photos accusing him of manipulating his own stature; he can be seen in photos wearing block heels, using a foot stool, or standing on his tiptoes. When it comes to perceived capabilities, it is fascinating to consider that people still value such superficial features.

Leadership effectiveness, as we try to believe and convince one another today, no longer has anything to do with an individual's physical characteristics. However, the importance of implicit preferences, such as those discussed above, often extend beyond what we might think. It is important that we recognize this as part of our journey towards gender equality awareness. It is therefore both logical and at the same time surprising that our unconscious associations are so deeply rooted and cannot be undone or erased overnight. We also see similar unconscious associations reflected in the contemporary anti-racism debate.

Research also shows a positive correlation between success and friendliness in regard to men, but a negative correlation in regard to women.[106] This means that, when a man is successful, he is considered to be friendly by both women and men; in direct contrast to this, a successful woman is considered to be less friendly by both sexes. In 2003 professors Frank Flynn and Cameron Anderson of Columbia Business School and New York University used using the case of Heidi Roizen to demonstrate this effect.

The case of Heidi Roizen

The case describes how an individual, Heidi Roizen, became a successful entrepreneur by using her outgoing personality and her professional network of influential people. Flynn and Anderson provided half of the students with the Heidi Roizen case. The other half were given the exact same case except for a single notable difference: they changed the name of the individual in the case from Heidi to Howard. The students' impression was that Heidi and Howard were equally competent, which seems appropriate as the cases they had been given were otherwise identical. However, though the students respected both Heidi and Howard, Heidi was seen by them as being somewhat egocentric and not the sort of person they would like to work with. Comparatively, Howard seemed to be a friendly colleague and an individual with whom people would like to work. The case shows how Heidi violated her stereotypical role as a woman, while Howard fulfilled his stereotypical role as a man and lived up to other people's expectations. As a result, people liked Howard, the male version of the character in the case study, but did not like Heidi, the female version.

Expectations (specifically, negative expectations) that are based on stereotypes that one has of an individual can interfere with the performance this person is expected to deliver. This interference is called a *stereotype threat*. In order to investigate and show this phenomenon, a study conducted at Stanford University, the University of Waterloo, and the University of Michigan tested women's mathematical skills by manipulating *stereotype threat.*[107] The researchers found that women who were confronted with their negative stereotype performed significantly worse than men who had achieved equivalent scores on previous unmanipulated tests. The study also found that this effect was eliminated when the women were told that no gender-based differences were expected among the maths-skills scores.

Studies investigating *stereotype threat* include an example of a study that found that white men perform worse on a math skills test when they thought they were competing with Asian men.[108] Similarly, African-American athletes were found to perform worse on a minigolf test when they were told beforehand that that the test would measure their 'sports intelligence'. However, when the same test was formulated as measuring 'natural athletic ability', white athletes performed worse compared with their African-American peers.[109] One of the consequences of *stereotype threat* is that stereotypes perpetuate themselves; this is because expectations based on these stereotypes are confirmed due to a 'self-fulfilling prophecy' – in other words, if an individual has a certain expectation, this expectation is more likely to become true.

Gender and self-confidence

One is not born, but rather becomes, a woman.
– Simone de Beauvoir (1908–1986), French philosopher, author, feminist

In 1920 Amelia Earhart (1897–1939) flew in an airplane for the first time, and from that moment on she only had one goal: to become a pilot. It was a decision that would alter the direction of her entire life. In 1932 Earhart became the first woman to fly a plane across the Atlantic Ocean, then, in 1935, she became the first person to fly solo across the Pacific Ocean. At the time, this achievement was, of course, both unique and unusual. However, this did not stop her from working hard to achieve what she wanted, nor relying on her own skills to do so. The confidence Earhart found in herself was one of her greatest incentives and motivations and led to her setting a number of records.

Confidence is the factor that turns thoughts into judgments about what we are capable of, and that then transforms those judgments into action.
– Richard Petty, professor of psychology at The Ohio State University

Furthermore, a study conducted by Zenger and Folkman revealed self-confidence to be as valuable as competence; self-confidence leads to action, attention, and resilience – all those qualities that Earhart needed to succeed in her flight across the Atlantic.

Yes, now little girls in Germany know they can become a hairdresser, or chancellor.
Let's see!
– Angela Merkel (1954), German politician, Chancellor since 2005

One study conducted by Cornell University revealed that a 'self-confidence gap' exists between men and women. Men were found to overestimate their own skills and achievements, while women were found to underestimate their own skills and achievements, despite the results of their actual performance being the same, both in regard to quality and quantity.[110]

A report by Hewlett Packard found that men apply for jobs and promotions even if they only meet 60 per cent of the necessary qualifications for the role; comparatively, women only apply when they meet 100 per cent of these qualifications. In addition, men are four times more likely than women to take the initiative to negotiate their salary and, when negotiating salary, women ask for 30 per cent less than men do. Finally, when college graduates were asked about their expected future earnings, female graduates reported an amount that was 20 per cent lower than that of their male peers.

These examples and research results show that becoming aware of our unconscious assumptions is an important step towards achieving gender equality in the workplace. Data from one LinkedIn survey shows that recruiters looking for candidates tend to open LinkedIn men's profiles more often than women's profiles. However, once recruiters have assessed a candidate's profile women and men often prove themselves to be equally suitable, and recruiters try and reach both candidates equally quickly. To avoid an initial selection bias, some organizations are now choosing to recruit individuals whose identities as of yet remain unknown to them (i.e. by anonymizing the candidate's name and photos), with some companies even using VR technology to avoid such bias.

Role model

I have had to learn that my voice has value. And if I don't use it, what's the point of
being in the room?
– Michelle Obama (1964), attorney, former first lady, and adviser to Barack
Obama, 44th President of the United States

The fact that male pilots dominated the aviation field did not stop Amelia Earhart from pursuing her dreams. It is important to know that sometimes self-confidence can be as valuable as competence; therefore you should not always wait for perfection and can consider applying for a job even if you do not meet all the necessary qualifications. Furthermore, if you are a female leader, try to be an example for other women. Women have fewer examples against which they can compare themselves, as well as fewer role models than men. It is important that women are aware of examples of successful women because, through such role models, these women can experiment with their own identities. As an organization, it is important to increase the presence and visibility of female leaders, but it is also important for woman to look for role models outside their own organization if there are few or no examples of female leaders within the organization itself.

As women move up hierarchical ladders within organizations, they become scarce. As a result of this they become increasingly visible and observed by other people. When this happens, women will start to focus more on their gender stereotypes, and consequently can become very concerned with how they come across to others in their organization. Part of the problem doubtless lies with other individuals having such a bias, but part of the solution also lies with the woman herself: she can learn to focus on herself and what she excels at in order to have confidence in her own abilities and potential. Research has shown that, for women, the very delicate gender bias manifesting within organizations and society disrupts the core learning cycle by which they might become leaders.[111]

As we saw earlier in this chapter, women often underestimate themselves while men tend to overestimate themselves, despite their actual performance being the same both quantitively and qualitatively. This bias is deeply rooted in our cultural definitions of gender – as well as in the positions women hold within society – and has far-reaching consequences. The aforementioned study by Zenger and Folkman shows that this difference is most prominent among women in their twenties and thirties and that, from the age of forty, women tend to become more self-confident. Younger women especially, those aged 20–30 years, may miss out on opportunities due to self-underestimation. For example, a 2016 report by Hewlett Packard in the magazine *PW* found that women in general, but especially young women, sometimes withdraw preventatively after applying for a job.[112]

The business case

As a woman, if you have doubts about your own skills and competences, then you should consider that research findings are very supportive and positive concerning the effects of female leadership. The conclusion based in the

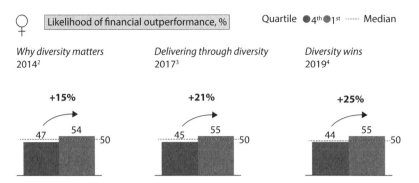

Figure 8.2: The business case for gender diversity studied by McKinsey over the past 6 years among 1,000 companies in 15 different countries. The percentages indicate the probability of higher financial performance. (Source: Consultancy.eu, 2020)

findings of McKinsey reports over recent years is unambiguous: companies make more profit if there are more women in leadership positions (see Figure 8.2).[113] Furthermore, Gallup indicates that female leaders generate higher **employee engagement** compared with male leaders,[114] while Zenger and Folkman emphasize that women do better than men in regard to their **leadership effectiveness.**[115]

That is why I want women in particular to know that they should trust themselves. Female managers: try to be a role model for others – embrace your achievements as well as your failures to aid your own development.

A 2011 study by Zenger and Folkman, which used a cohort of 7,280 leaders from successful organizations (including profit and non-profit, local, and international), shows the differences between men and women regarding leadership effectiveness. The findings of the study were so significant they were reported in the world press. A 2012 prime-time FOX News broadcast, wherein Jack Zenger was asked to account for the exceptional results of his research, exemplifies the attention this research study received. Among other things, the study showed that men occupied most of the top positions among those organizations included in the research. Some particularly interesting facts emerged when the researchers focused on the qualitative data pertaining to the differences between men and women. Most gender-related stereotypes lead us to believe that female leaders will excel in social and caring skills, skills such as building relationships and showing integrity. While the data showed that the female leaders in the study scored higher than the men regarding these skills, they also revealed that female leaders excelled at far more than these 'traditional female skills'. In fact, women achieved a higher rating for 12 out of the 16 surveyed leadership competencies when compared with their male colleagues. The two competencies where women showed the greatest positive distinction from males were the *take initiative* and *achieve results* competencies. These two competencies precisely represent those skills with the strongest associations to 'traditional male competences'.

In 2017, the same study was repeated among 51,418 leaders worldwide, and yielded even more interesting findings than the first. It emerged that what distinguishes women leaders from their male peers in such a positive manner can be expressed in ten behaviours (see the box below). Moreover, we see that these behaviours, which positively distinguish women from men, recur across all sectors.

What positively distinguishes women

1. Always willing to do more than merely what needs to be done.
2. Always approachable about agreements made.
3. Careful to honour agreements made.
4. Energetic in challenging targets.
5. Providing the group with a high level of energy and enthusiasm.
6. Sincerely focused on the development of others.
7. Actively looking for opportunities to get feedback in order to improve themselves.
8. Staying in touch with personal issues and individual problems of team members.
9. Keeping goals in mind and ensuring that targets are met successfully.
10. Being committed to improvement based on feedback from others.

When looking closely at those behaviours described in the previous chapters, we recognize them as being desirable in our present time because they help organizations achieve better results through leadership. Is it perhaps from among this list of behaviours, which distinguish women most positively, that we will find the summary of behaviours needed in our search for leadership transformation?

Male/female leadership in education

For 6 years, Academica has been collecting 360-degree feedback data from more than 1,150 Dutch education leaders based on the Zenger and Folkman's assessment method.[116] In this way, more than 25,000 feedback scores were collected from the managers (the supervisors of these educational leaders), employees (people directly supervised by the leaders), colleagues (people of the same hierarchical position as the leaders), and other professionals

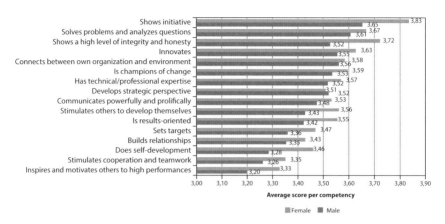

Figure 8.3: Scores for Dutch education leaders, divided per men–women. (Source: Research Academica, 2018)

from within direct environments of the leaders themselves. The profile differences between the male and female Dutch education leaders were also examined as part of the analysis of these data. The differences between men and women were even more evident in this study than they are outside of the educational sector. Women scored better than their male peers did on no fewer than 15 of the 16 competences investigated (see Figure 8.3). Only for the *develops strategic perspective* competency did men achieve a higher average score than their female peers.

This study also looked at the employee engagement scores of the education leaders and, remarkably, found no difference between men and women. In general, however, we do see a correlation between higher effectiveness scores and higher employee engagement scores. A study among 154 school leaders in primary education (as conducted by Kwanten,[117] and discussed earlier in Chapter 1) revealed that students' learning outcomes improved when engagement was higher. However, the study also found that men and women exhibited different behaviours than men when trying to increase employee engagement.

When taking a closer look at the research, another striking finding can be seen in regard to the 10 per cent of leaders who scored best (according to the leaders' total leadership effectiveness scores among the overall research population of 1,150 leaders in the Academica study): 29.5 per cent of the 'top 10 per cent' of leaders' in the database were men, while roughly 61.6 per cent were women (see Figure 8.4). The gender of the remaining 8.9 per cent of leaders remains unknown (as it was not filled in on the questionnaire). The fact that there is such a high share of female leaders from among the 'top 10 per cent' of leaders is certainly remarkable, especially since the total

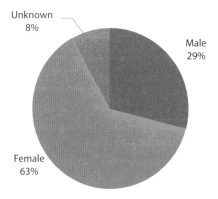

Figure 8.4: Percentage of men to women in the
top 10 percent highest scoring leaders.
(Research Academica, 2018)

number of men and women in the research population was almost equal. Accordingly, this difference can therefore not be explained by a greater number of women in the total research population.

We see that the impact of leadership in education can be described as follows: better school leaders create higher employee engagement, which itself has a direct impact on the students and their parents and, subsequently, on the students' learning performance (as described in Chapter 1 and Figure 1.4). Both men and women show their strengths in this regard although, according to the numbers, we see women doing this more vigorously.

Gender and our challenge

A study by Korn Ferry,[118] conducted among 55,000 professionals in 90 countries, is often cited as evidence that women score higher than men on almost all emotional intelligence competencies (11 out of 12). The subject of emotional intelligence was a very popular for a number of years, but it also remains a highly debated one. According to the Korn Ferry study, women were 86 per cent more likely than men to show the *emotional self-awareness* competency, and furthermore were 45 per cent more likely to exhibit the *empathy* competency. Women also performed better on competencies such as coaching, inspirational leadership, conflict management, organizational self-awareness, adaptability, teamwork, and performance orientation.

Certain other studies often show that women value relation-building interactions more than men do; something that is also confirmed by the Korn Ferry study. However, as the Belgian sociologist Veerle Draulans describes in her research report, *Glazen plafond: realiteit of mythe?* ('Glass ceiling: reality or myth'), the effect of these other studies is seen in how, in our current society, we increasingly find and are convinced that women are different and have a different leadership style than men.[119] We see that we are talking more and more about typically feminine aspects and characteristics, and that we are increasingly meeting, addressing, and acting on the call for greater feminine attention when it comes to understanding and interacting with one another. Draulans describes this emphasis and attention as 'feminine colour' because we have agreed that the twenty-first century will be the 'century of the feminine'. However, we must be careful not to prejudge ourselves in our pursuit of certain desired outcomes, for instance by thinking: 'If only we have more women at the top of the board, everything will improve'. We must remember that we are all subject to those contexts in which we see and want to see things.

According to Forbes coach, Carı Coath, four competencies are recognizable in those leaders who are able to successfully connect with their employees (see the box below). Interestingly, these behaviours are often those that set women apart from men, even though women themselves often have a lot to learn. This issue remains a challenge for both sexes.

Competencies of leaders who connect

Self-awareness

These leaders are aware of their own motivations and emotions and can under-stand and can furthermore accept these motivations and emotions. They are able to receive feedback without reacting defensively. It is important that you become aware of your own reactions and emotions if you want to further deve-lop this skill, especially when engaging in emotionally charged discussions.

Transparency

These leaders ensure that vulnerabilities and mistakes of both the leader and the employee can be discussed. By being transparent about these matters, peo-ple can improve themselves together.

Presence

Leaders who are present can better observe and appreciate the emotions of other people. These leaders recognize the emotional needs of others and can deal with them empathetically.

> **Self-control**
> These leaders are not drawn into emotional reactions. They remain in control and can choose how they respond to a particular situation at a particular time.

Following this discussion of all those studies on the differences between men and women – which even showed positive results for women regarding their competence profiles and business barometers – it is now time to look at the those facts and data that pertaining to the workplace, and consider how we might organize the workplace in such a way that favours the participation of women. We are becoming increasingly convinced that we should make more use of women's potential in the workplace. The 2015 McKinsey Global Institute report, *The Power of Parity*, indicates that if we were to make greater use of the talents of women globally, then this would yield an increase of 12 trillion USD in the global gross domestic product by 2025.[120] Despite the benefits that arise from a higher participation of women in leadership positions, and despite the fact that Dutch society is generally progressive in the field of gender equality, this gender equality is unfortunately not yet reflected in the Dutch labour market.

According to a more recent study by McKinsey, the Netherlands scores well on three social indicators of gender equality: legal protection, digital inclusion, and financial inclusion.[121] Furthermore, women have a strong position in education within the Netherlands, with women under the age of 45 often having a higher level of education than their male peers.

When it comes to an equal division between men and women within the labour market, however, the Netherlands still lags behind. Despite many initiatives, the potential of many women within the Dutch labour market has yet to be fully utilized, something that becomes even clearer when the situation in the Netherlands is compared with that of other Western European countries. In fact, we see a high degree of inequality in nine out of the fifteen gender-equality indicators relating to the Dutch labour market (see Figure 8.5).

According to the study by McKinsey, of the Western European Nations, the Netherlands scores the lowest on the following gender-equality indicators:

– **Number of paid working hours**
   The average number of paid working hours for Dutch women is 71 per cent of that of the paid working hours for men; in Western Europe this average is 79 per cent.
– **Average monthly income**
   The average monthly income for Dutch women is 61 per cent of that of men; in Western Europe this average is 68 per cent.

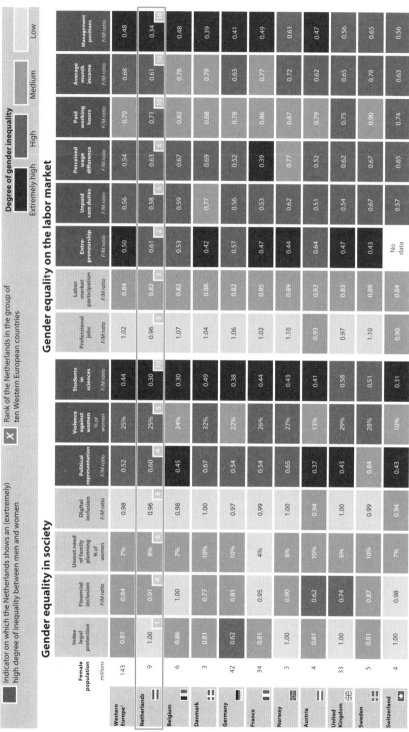

Figure 8.5: Dutch gender-equality scores indicate a high or extremely high degree of inequality in 9 out of the 15 indicators. (Source: Graven & Krishnan, 2018)

- **Representation in management positions**
  The average share of women in management positions in the Netherlands is 25 per cent; in Western Europe this average is 48 per cent.
- **Students in beta (science and technology) courses.**
  The average share of women in science education programmes in the Netherlands is 23 per cent; in Western Europe this average share is 31 per cent.

Accordingly, within the Netherlands women perform well in the education sector, while their participation in the labour market as a whole is also relatively high. However, they work fewer hours on average than men and their gross domestic product (GDP) is also lower than that of men. The system explaining this situation appears to be self-perpetuating and comprises three dimensions:

- **Uneven spread across sectors**
  The majority of working women work part-time and therefore make a relatively low contribution compared to the full-time equivalent.
- **Unequal distribution of paid work and unpaid care**
  There is an unequal division of paid work and unpaid care (for example, childcare or informal care of sick friends or relations).
- **Pronounced views on social norms**
  Views on social norms contribute to the maintenance of prejudices and stereotypes that negatively influence equal distribution between men and women.

The way in which men and women compare to one another regarding the division of roles in the workplace and in society is still significantly bound to dated images about what our society needs, as well as how men and women play a role in relation to these needs. Ideas about what is normal and/or desired within society endure and can remain the same for years, decades, and sometimes even centuries. The only way to break this outdated division of roles is by focusing and positively using your own energy to improve the situation at hand. It is where we manage to find common focus that this shift will come about.

Summary: We must be aware of the influence of gender bias and stereotypes when it comes to opportunities for women. Female leaders can become far more prominent and visible by taking action themselves and by making their voices heard, but they must also be supported when doing so by their organization. Clear agreements are essential to changing together: nothing happens by itself. In this regard, standardization may prove to be the best answer after all, but above all else: inspire, motivate, and offer opportunities for women to develop their strengths.

Motivational quotes from inspiring women

Have the courage to stand up, and focus on your current job and do it very well.
– Indra Nooyi, chairman and CEO PepsiCo

Go do what you really enjoy doing, and find the best school to train you.
– Meg Withman, CEO Hewlett Packard

Don't see it as work, see it as a platform to send a message.
– Oprah Winfrey, CEO Oprah Winfrey Network

Don't look back, impact the community now.
– Angela Ahrendts, senior VP Apple Retail

Get better in what you do, and take it step by step.
– Maria Bartiromo, FOX Network anchor

I knew what kind of woman I wanted to be, I wanted to independent.
– Diane von Furstenberg, fashion designer, entrepreneur, philanthropist

Figure out what you want to do but be flexible in your mind.
– Carla Harris, vice chairman and managing director, Morgan Stanley

There is no limit to what we, as women, can accomplish.
– Michelle Obama

In the future there will be no female leaders. There will be just leaders.
– Sheryl Sandberg

Emancipation is you being at the steering wheel of your own life.
– Queen Máxima of The Netherlands

The male–female views and generational discussions are a good prelude to introducing the last substantive theme. Inclusive thinking should not be restricted to just talking, it should lead to action. That is why the next chapter is explicitly about inclusive leadership.

Confucius | 551 BCE–479 BCE

Niccolò Machiavelli | 1469-1527

Thomas Carlyle | 1795-1881

Frederick Taylor | 1856-1915

Max Weber | 1864-1920

Bertrand Russell | 1872-1970

Simone de Beauvoir | 1908-1986

Abraham Maslow | 1908-1970

Peter Drucker | 1909-2005

John W. Gardner | 1912-2002

Nelson Mandela | 1918-2013

Thomas Kuhn | 1922-1996

Jim Rohn | 1930-2009

Jack Zenger | 1931

Umberto Eco | 1932-2016

Jack Welch | 1935-2020

Richard Petty | 1937

Jesse Jackson | 1941 *Inclusion is not a matter of political correctness. It is the key to growth.*

Stephen Kern | 1943

Daniel Goleman | 1946

Anders Ericsson | 1947-2020

John C. Maxwell | 1947

Peter Senge | 1947

Jaap van Muijen | 1960

Otto Scharmer | 1961

Paul J. Zak | 1962

Frederic Laloux | 1969

9.　Inclusive leadership

Inclusion is not a matter of political correctness. It is the key to growth.
– Jesse Jackson (1941), politician, pastor, and civil rights activist

After the death of George Floyd in May 2020 due to police brutality, the Black Lives Matter movement became more prominent and more in the spotlights than ever before. Accordingly, we increasingly come to realize that 'change has to come about **now**'.[122] We are done with ethnic profiling and its social consequences, and the questions we are increasingly asking ourselves are: Can we acknowledge our behaviour with regard to diversity, and do we recognize the consequences of this behaviour? Do we want to change our behaviour and how should enact this change? It is time to take action; in order to be open to our differences, we must be able to change our course. This is something we have known about for some time when speaking about inclusive leadership.

Demographic developments resulting from migration and immigration, among other things, offer plenty of diversity in society, and there are many opportunities by which we can fully benefit from this diversity. We have a diverse workforce at our disposal, and various research studies show the benefits of diversity in the workplace. For example, diversity in the workforce is associated with improved performance levels throughout the organization as a whole. Following on from the business case for increased gender diversity presented in the previous chapter, McKinsey research from 2020 also shows a stable business case over the past 6 years for ethnic and cultural diversity. From the 1,000 companies across 15 different countries that were studied, it was found that those companies that scored in the top quartile in terms of profitability performed 36 per cent better than those in the bottom quartile. Furthermore, it was found that greater cultural and ethnic diversity within the organization offers an even greater likelihood of above-average profitability compared with those figures presented in the previous chapter on gender diversity (see Figure 9.1).

The most prominent author specializing in this issue in the Netherlands is Saniye Çelik, who expounds on the business case for diversity in public organizations while also considering various perspectives on diversity.[123] Çelik also underlines the need to work towards an inclusive culture. Accordingly, four common drivers emerge from an inclusive culture: equality, legitimacy, creativity,[124] and connection.[125]

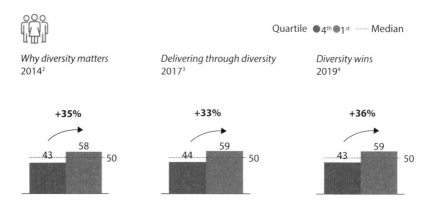

Figure 9.1: The business case over 6 years for ethnic and cultural diversity according to McKinsey. (Source: Consultancy.eu, 2020)

However, we also see that diversity in working environments exposes the differences between people, something that may potentially damage the sense of connectedness, appreciation, and opportunity therein. In our current society, we see increasing evidence that people's success often depends on their diversity characteristics, such as their gender, race, and ethnicity. Many researchers therefore argue for careful attention to the effects of diversity.[126] We see that, in finding sufficient staff for their organization, many employers now see diversity as a necessary experiment and challenge. Diversity in the workforce is therefore not shown to be an obstacle, but rather something that can be used to promote the employer. Despite this progress in understanding, advancing and fostering inclusion remains slow. This process towards inclusion in the workplace is described by the American Kristina Bourne (2009) as 'a powerful transformation of an organization's culture to one in which every individual is valued as a vital component of the organization's success and competitive advantage' (p. 263).

Inclusion and diversity

Inclusion is the involvement of disadvantaged groups in society based on equal rights and obligations. (Source: Wikipedia)

According to the Oxford English Dictionary, diversity comprises both variety and variation, and can refer can refer to economics, law, sociology, politics, art, culture, science, and technology.

The use of the word 'diversity' often refers to what we formally call 'multiculturalism'.

Multiculturalism is a social and political position that presupposes equality among different cultural, ethnic and religious communities within a defined administrative area. (Source: Wikipedia)

We use terms such as 'inclusion' and 'inclusive policy', and 'diversity' and 'diversity management' to deal with diversity in a constructive manner regarding workplaces in labour organizations.

In this context, diversity policy refers to those policies aimed at recognizing and valuing differences between people. Inclusion does not only look at connectedness within the organization, as diversity does, but rather seeks a balance between connectedness and the unique characteristics of the individual. Inclusive leadership is an invitation to develop an attitude that is fully accepting of others, including all their strengths and weaknesses, thereby enabling everyone to make progress.

This inclusive culture of connectedness and equality seems to be gaining more meaning in our daily lives with the outbreak of COVID-19. As a result we are more likely to act, pay greater attention to one another, and try to help others who can no longer take care of themselves. This demonstrates that, while diversity is an established fact in both organizations and in society, inclusion remains an individual choice.[127]

As the diversity field has evolved, scientists have become increasingly focused on promoting the potential value of diversity for diverse work processes and organizational mechanisms.[128] For example, Agrawal (2012) describes some factors to which diversity can refer, such as age, gender, culture, education, employee status, physical appearance, family composition, regional origin, national origin, ways of thinking, religion, and race, among others. Past studies are dominated by a focus on the 'problems' that can arise from diversity.[129] For example, diversity could cause or inflame negative behaviour and create affective outcomes such as reduced social cohesion, relational conflicts, and higher staff turnover as a result of perceived differences between employees and unsettled stereotypes about employees.[130]

However, many early studies also show the competitive advantage brought about by a heterogeneous workforce which, according to Jackson et al. (1991), positively stimulates tasks requiring creativity and judgment. Furthermore, positive complications brought about by diversity are often acknowledged in terms of cognitive outcomes; accordingly, diversity allows employees from different social backgrounds to contribute more to innovation, ideas, and creativity. A particular stream within this research field investigates work environments in which different individuals feel included.[131]

The *optimal distinctiveness theory* explains that people need uniqueness and individualization on the one hand, and a degree of inclusion and connectedness on the other. Tensions between uniqueness and connectedness is an underlying theme in this inclusion and diversity literature, and both argue that certain demographic groups have fewer chances by which they can belong to 'valued' groups. These 'valued' groups tend to occupy higher positions within an organization due to the characteristics that often belong to those individuals who occupy such positions.

Your uniqueness is therefore judged according to the 'value' of your characteristics. A concrete example of this is a person who is able to recover hacked software during a time that is increasingly troubled by 'computer hacks'; this individual then becomes highly valued within their organization.

Yet diversity theories only emphasize the benefits of similarity by focusing solely on one side of the coin: the theme of connectedness. This is also evident from various research results whereby the focus on connectedness is often counterproductive, suggesting the possibility that demographic similarities do not always create a sense of connectedness and that they therefore do not sufficiently lead to positive results within the organization.[132] The inequality of opportunity lies precisely in the appreciation of uniqueness. Therefore, according to a study by Shore et al. (2011), connectedness must be accompanied by appreciation for the uniqueness of individuals for promoting the perception of employee inclusion. Such perceptions, such as meeting human needs, togetherness, and uniqueness, should provide more consistent results for the organization.

Leaders have an impact on inclusion

In organizations themselves, inclusion can be defined as *the degree to which an employee feels that he or she is a valued member of a whole*. According to this definition, the focus is on finding a balance between inclusion and uniqueness. The traditional approach has been to recruit and hire diverse employees in order to create cohesion between diversity and inclusion.[133] Until recently, little research had been done on the internal organizational processes that generate inclusion, beyond promoting purely numerical representations of diversity. However, researchers are increasingly recognizing the importance of the internal organizational processes that hold leaders responsible for creating diversity and equal opportunities at work.[134] After all, leaders are able to directly influence the way in which work is organized in order to promote or undermine inclusion.[135]

In her 2015 PhD research on leadership and inclusivity in public organizations, Tanachia Ashikali describes what an inclusive leader does:[136]

– Inclusive leadership encourages the appreciation and exchange of different backgrounds, perspectives, and ideas held by the various team members.
– The leader ensures that there is a safe environment within a team, one in which each team member can present and have their ideas heard. In other words, each team member feels at ease in the team and can be themselves.
– In addition, by expressing their appreciation for diversity, the leader shows that each team member is a valued part of the whole.

Fair treatment from leaders towards individual members within an organization leads these members to feel as if they are more respected in the group.[137] When fair procedures are used consistently across the group, members can take pride in group membership. In contrast, unfair treatment of group members – causing these individuals and potentially the group as a whole to not feel respected – leads to psychological withdrawal from, and low identification with, the group or organization.[138]

Leaders can have a strong impact on the experience of employees within a team, especially as part of a diverse team in which different values and perspectives can coexist. Douglas et al. (2003) argue that leaders of diverse groups should exhibit behaviours that are consistent with those group values that create a dual focus: acceptance of diverse members, and appropriate behaviours necessary to achieve group goals. Leadership behaviour such as this contributes to a group environment in which all members can develop and improve. Likewise, Wasserman et al. (2008) highlights the importance of leaders creating an organizational culture of inclusion. Leaders who support a culture of inclusion tend to avoid resisting efforts towards diversification. Such a culture of inclusion can create a learning opportunity for the leader so that efforts towards diversification are more successful.

Another important research finding that demonstrates the importance of inclusive leadership within an organization is that such leadership holds a positive correlation with employee satisfaction and engagement.[139] Employees who feel more socially integrated within their organization are more likely to identify and bond with that organization; consequently, they are also less likely to leave. Inclusion also has a positive effect on the career opportunities of all employees. As we saw in Chapter 8, a woman can encounter many obstacles throughout their career as compared with the average (white) man. We see similar obstacles facing employees of diverse origins in regard to their careers.[140]

For example we see that, compared to white men, black men must work far longer after leaving school, while Latino workers have to accrue many more years with their current employer in order to receive equivalent promotion opportunities compared with their white peers.[141] Arguably, these results may indicate that individuals of lower status (women, minorities) are more strictly and harshly assessed when it comes to their norms and qualifications. They have to prove themselves more in regard to their competencies when compared with individuals of a higher status (white men).[142] Inclusion makes it possible to stimulate and confirm the unique contribution of individuals, creating greater equality of opportunities in a work environment with diversity.

How can a leader achieve inclusion?

A study conducted by Deloitte Australia among inclusive leaders from Australia, New Zealand, Singapore, Hong Kong, Canada, and the United States shows that such inclusive leaders possess six fundamental attributes that stimulate inclusive mindsets and behaviours in this rapidly changing world: commitment, courage, knowledge of bias, curiosity, cultural intelligence, and collaboration. These attributes enable leaders and managers to deal much more effectively with a wide range of culturally, demographically, and behaviourally diverse people. They also help leaders gain access to a broader spectrum of ideas and perspectives, which can improve their decision making, as well as their ability to innovate, deal with uncertainty, and anticipate the future. Especially in uncertain times – such as the current COVID-19 pandemic – a lack of control and the spread of misinformation increases the risk of bias, xenophobia, and racism that can impact people in the workplace and beyond. By cultivating and practicing the six signature traits, leaders can foster a more inclusive workplace environment in the face of COVID-19, both today and in the long term.

At an international level an increasing number of companies are, like Deloitte, trying to create an inclusive working environment in which everyone is welcome and where everyone can be themselves. The furniture company IKEA is one of the top 10 employers for promoting diversity and inclusion within the company. At IKEA, inclusion is about creating a work environment wherein all employees are successful because they feel welcome, respected, supported, and valued. An inclusive work environment is about developing an inclusive culture, and engaging in inclusive behaviour on a daily basis in order to make the most of differences between individuals. In the case of IKEA, this is achieved through workshops. During these workshops, benefits and possible barriers are discussed with top leaders and managers from all countries and, following these discussions, equality targets are set, and a diversity plan that contributes to the creation of an inclusive culture is developed.

It is clear that the leader plays an important role in the organization and realization of inclusion within their own organization, but how exactly are leaders themselves to achieve these ends? Four points of attention can be identified if we consider the example of Deloitte, which support the lessons learned by findings from various related studies (see box for an elaboration).

– First, we are discussing a leader's knowledge of the world, our different cultures and customs, and so-called global leadership.
– Second, the ability to focus on real collaboration between people and, therefore, within teams.
– Third, self-awareness about your own way of acting and behaving, the effect of these traits on other people, and willingness to learn from this effect accordingly.
– Fourthly and finally, what we can call 'cultural intelligence'. To what extent are you able to adapt to a new cultural environment?

Four points of attention by which a leader can achieve inclusion

Global leadership

Inclusive leadership requires leaders with global knowledge and skills. These skills are an essential part of a global mindset, enabling one to use global logic in order to understand differences in leadership practices.[143] Jokinen (2005) defined this global leadership competence as a set of universal qualities or characteristics that enable individuals to perform well outside their own national organizational culture, regardless of their educational or ethnic background, or whichever field is described in their job description.

Collaboration

Inclusive leadership is a team process in which, according to Kouzes and Posner (2012), collaboration is a crucial competence for achieving and maintaining high performance. The more diverse organizations become, the more essential collaboration skills will be in anticipating conflicting interests and natural tensions.

Self-awareness

Alongside collaborative working and having a global mentality, emotional self-awareness is a further crucial component for realizing success.[144] Self-awareness of your leadership style is an essential first step in identifying key strengths and areas for improvement, as well as for creating a successful development action plan. According to Mavrinac (2005), self-awareness leads to reflection and insight which, in turn, lead to development and change.

Cultural intelligence

Inclusive leadership also focuses on what is called 'cultural intelligence'. This intelligence does not only encompass cultural awareness and sensitivity, but furthermore the ability of an individual to successfully adapt to new and un-known cultural institutions, that is, the ability to function effectively in environments characterized by cultural diversity.[145] Earkey and Peterson (2004) argue that cultural intelligence reflects a person's capacity to adapt to cultures, and to collect, interpret, as well as to act on 'radically different' cultures and/or environments.

Inclusive leaders succeed in building diverse relationships by focusing on these four areas. They understand that through recognition, appreciation, and by paying attention, you will increase other people's confidence in you as a professional and as a leader. With the constant pressure to change in today's social and business ecosystems, our leaders must assume a completely new mindset, toolset, and skillset.[146] Inclusive leadership is a positive breeding ground for creating socially just organizations in which all staff, community members, and stakeholders involved in organizational processes are seen as meaningful participants. Accordingly, inclusive leadership is not just about integrating marginalized groups purely for the sake of meeting targets or to bring about financial benefits, it is also because –as we become increasingly interconnected – there will always be differences between people within organizations.[147]

Summary: A diverse work environment can lead to differences in opportunities and possibilities between individuals. Inclusive leadership focuses on a balance between experiencing connectedness and the uniqueness of individuals; it also emphasizes the importance of appreciation, and highlights the need to develop global leadership competencies that enable leaders to reap the benefits that emerge from a diverse work environment. As a result, inclusive leadership is no longer a matter of simply recruiting and hiring diverse employees, rather, it is about recognizing everyone's unique contribution to the organization.

Now is the time to appraise and organize the direction of your impact. Chapter 10 gives you the final support you need to do this.

190

Success always depends on careful preparation; without that preparation, failure is a fact.

The best leaders are loved and feared, but because it is difficult to unite both in one person, the next best option is to be feared as a leader.

The history of the world is but the biography of great men.

In the past the man has been first; in the future the system must be first.

Charismatic leadership is authority based on the leader's personal qualities and the recognition thereof by their followers.

The whole problem with the world is that fools and fanatics are always so certain of themselves, and wiser people so full of doubt.

One is not born, but rather becomes, a woman.

If you only have a hammer, you tend to see every problem as a nail.

Culture eats strategy for breakfast.

The fundamental task of management is to make people capable of joint performance through common goals, common values, the right structure, and the training and development they need to perform and to respond to change.

The only way to discover your strengths is through feedback analysis.

Pity the leader caught between unloving critics and uncritical lovers.

May your choices reflect your hopes, not your fears.

We see the world in terms of our theories.

The enemy of great is good.

Greatness is not caused by the absence of weakness.

Inspirational leadership is not about a single ingredient; it is all about the recipe. It comes about by combining ingredients.

I belong to a lost generation and am comfortable only in the company of others who are lost and lonely.

If you want to change the culture of an organization, change the way it develops its leaders

Confidence is the factor that turns thoughts into judgments about what we are capable of, and that then transforms those judgments into action.

Inclusion is not a matter of political correctness. It is the key to growth.

Humanity has never strived to slow down.

People need to be smarter with their emotions.

Deliberate Practice makes perfect.

Leadership is not about titles, positions, or flowcharts. It is about one life influencing another

A learning organization is an organization that is continually expanding its capacity to create its future.

Leadership is shaped in the process between the personality of the leader, the characteristics of the followers, and those of the situation.

The business that leaders are in today, is the business of transforming awareness... There is deep longing for more meaning, for connections.

Trust is kind of this economic lubricant. When trust is high, morale is high... Higher trust environments produce individuals who are happier.

In the new organizations, management is becoming a way to really bring out the best in people, where trust is given and where humanity is the focus. This ensures work environments that are inspired, goal-oriented and productive.

Confucius | 551 BCE–479 BCE
Niccolò Machiavelli | 1469-1527
Thomas Carlyle | 1795-1881
Frederick Taylor | 1856-1915
Max Weber | 1864-1920
Bertrand Russell | 1872-1970
Simone de Beauvoir | 1908-1986
Abraham Maslow | 1908-1970
Peter Drucker | 1909-2005
John W. Gardner | 1912-2002
Nelson Mandela | 1918-2013
Thomas Kuhn | 1922-1996
Jim Rohn | 1930-2009
Jack Zenger | 1931
Umberto Eco | 1932-2016
Jack Welch | 1935-2020
Richard Petty | 1937
Jesse Jackson | 1941
Stephen Kern | 1943
Daniel Goleman | 1946
Anders Ericsson | 1947-2020
John C. Maxwell | 1947
Peter Senge | 1947
Jaap van Muijen | 1960
Otto Scharmer | 1961
Paul J. Zak | 1962
Frederic Laloux | 1969

10. Making Shift Happen!

Now is the time to act using both your **strength** and your **passion**. Leadership is about making choices; be aware of, take control of, and direct your own impact. Be proactive: you do not have to wait for someone else to ask you to act or make a change. A day without action is a day wasted; and, to offer you my father's mantra once more, remember: 'Don't get annoyed, just marvel'.

To help you on your way, I close this book with concluding suggestions and recommendations for actions to be taken.

– Appearances are contagious. Your knowledge is essential, but how you use this knowledge in all your expressions determines your ability to include people in your team. Even if you have never met someone, your reputation will nevertheless precede you. The good news here is that you can influence this reputation by taking control and directing your impact.

Be aware of your appearance and focus on what you want to achieve. Make sure that in all your expressions you ensure consistent and supportive behaviour. Remember that the repetition of your message is essential, and be open to the feedback others give you.

– There is good news for all of us: we are all capable of learning leadership. Furthermore, if we learn leadership purposefully and with focus and persistence, we will achieve more. Not only individuals but also organizations are able to learn, however, we all have to take an active attitude in this; both to sense and to respond. If we want to change organizations, we will have to change our leadership and our prevailing views about leadership. The involvement of people from all levels within the organization is essential for this process.

Formulate your goals with a meaning that extends beyond merely the desired turnover or the project aim of the day. It is important that you contribute as a person, and that you fully understand your ability to do so. Ask yourself the following questions: What impact would I like to have? How can I test and compare this impact? When do I and my environment experience this impact? How can I actively involve my manager in my development objectives?

–   Focusing on what you already do very well but that you could do even
    better is a process that has a more powerful result than merely striving
    for small improvements. Remember: nobody is perfect! The so-called
    CPO model (Competence – Passion – Organizational Needs) will support
    you in analysing your sweet spot. If you focus on and use your strength
    as a starting point, and do so with both enjoyment and impact, you
    will be the first to benefit. Even better, your environment will also
    benefit from this process. Extraordinary achievements may emerge as
    engagement within your organization grows.

Critically analyse yourself and ask yourself questions: Am I in my sweet spot?
Do I get energy from what I do? Do I understand what my contribution is? What
do my team and organization need? What am I good at? Am I focusing on my
strength, or am I always working on improving my weaknesses?

–   Inspiring and motivating others is also called the 'silver bullet' of
    leadership success. There are several ways to inspire and motivate
    other individuals. The way you choose to do this depends on your
    situation and the way from which you can draw the most strength. High
    performing organizations work from a clear vision whereby leadership
    guides individuals in a process of continuous development so they are
    able to achieve better performance. The right balance between fast and
    qualitative action is hereby achieved.

Undertake the following analysis for yourself: How do I respond to problems
or trends in the market or sector? What vision or view do I base myself on?
Am I quick to organize necessary changes? Do I discuss these changes with
the team? Do I ensure that people from all levels in the organization can
discuss these changes and understand them? Am I focused on developing
my people?

–   Achieving results with an engaged team means that you must ensure
    that there is open and clear communication about the course of the
    organization, and that you lead people in pursuing this course. This
    all emerges from an open attitude that lets professionals self-direct
    the deployment and utilization of their own qualities in order to meet
    organizational objectives. You must express that you are open to learn
    and should support your team as much as possible in their development.
    Trust is the incentive and driver of shift and change. Do others in your
    team dare to take these steps towards change with you?

Together with your team, try and analyse how you experience your team dynamics. Ask yourself: Am I consistent in my behaviour and my expressions towards other members in the team? Am I aware of the utilization of my own expertise? What do people say about me? Is my attitude positive? Am I teachable and open to learning thigs? Do I encourage people to talk? How do I deal with feedback? Do I give my professionals feedback?

– If you want to transform the organization, you will have to start making changes together with all the professionals across every layer of the organization. Your leadership style has a direct impact on the culture and, therefore, the results of the organization. Developing yourself is not an activity that can be learned through schooling, it takes place in the workplace itself. Consider whether you involve all the people around you in your development and ensure that you support each other in this process. Knowledge about other people within the organization and your attitude towards them is the key to realizing constant mutual development. Transformation concerns the individual, the team, and the organization in accordance with a long-term vision of the contribution you want to make to society.

What then do I want to focus on? Do I want to focus on managing and maintaining, or on improving? What do I want to stimulate my team members to do – to improve or to carry out necessary activities? Am I open in my attitude towards others? What is my own perspective and vision concerning the contribution of our organization to society? Am I open regarding what I want to change about myself and do I also involve other people in this regard?

– Asking and giving feedback is an essential skill for leaders and all professionals within organizations. The more we ask for and give feedback to one another, the better we will be able to develop ourselves, and thus achieve better results together. Increasing our awareness of how we can use our knowledge and skills for our organization is an important first step in this process. It is not an easy task but we will be able to increase our effectiveness by predominantly providing more reinforcing feedback and, where necessary, redirecting feedback.

Create an atmosphere in which people are curious about one another. What do people know about my expertise and development goals, and what do I know about those of my colleagues? How often do I give feedback to other professionals and my colleagues? What kind of feedback do I give – reinforcing or redirecting? Am I sincerely interested in the other person? Am I positive about my employees?

– Four generations in the workplace means different views and expectations. Millennials are increasingly assuming their turn in the driving seat when it comes to leadership. Our challenge is to transition to new forms of living and working together, forms in which we involve all generations. The shift from ego to eco becomes increasingly noticeable; meanwhile meaningfulness itself becomes more important, something that is also reflected in the organization's goals. Every person needs attention and feedback to make this shift happen. The youngest generations are seeking this in an even more concrete manner by asking for redirecting and honest feedback. As with any young employee, there is uncertainty concerning their own skills.

Analyse the team and what stereotypical views you and your team members have of the various generations therein. To which generation do I pay more attention? How do I deal with the differences between people? Am I using my knowledge of the potentially different needs and experiences of these generations to better get to know my fellow team members, so that we may better complement one other, or am I using this to emphasize their differences? Do I create a culture in which I also give good and efficacious feedback to the youngest generation?

– In leadership, we deal with ingrained patterns of thinking as to what is typically male and what is typically female. This becomes clear in all kinds of ways when we consider and discuss successful leadership in men and women, as well as the behaviours that go with this leadership. However, these patterns of thinking are also reflected in the participation rate of women at different organizational levels and across all sectors, especially in regard to those positions in which the responsibilities assigned are of the highest level. Research shows that women, globally and in all sectors, are doing a fantastic job, and are achieving successful results with their leadership. Not fully utilizing the potential of women's leadership is therefore no longer an option. The challenge now lies in the way in which we bridge this gap together. At this time in which we need to achieve change together, every effort will be needed.

What percentage of top management positions in my organization are filled by women? What kind of actions are taken within the organization to help develop women at all levels of the organization? Do I have any idea of this potential within the organization? What kind of networks are used both within and without the organization in order to recognize and develop one another's qualities? What can I do myself in order to develop and keep developing? How do I position female colleagues?

– Our organizations reflect our society. While on the one hand diversity in the workplace exposes the differences between people, it also offers opportunities for us to connect, to appreciate, and to develop. Our success as a person within an organization – and the consequent success of the organization itself as a result – is to utilize and expand the unique strength of every individual in regard to coherence and connectedness in the pursuit of a common organizational goal. Inclusive leadership is necessary in order to achieve this goal.

What does the distribution of my team look like when I consider it from a perspective of diversity? What do I do to give everyone in the organization a sense of appreciation? How do I support the exchange of ideas and backgrounds? What do I know about the different backgrounds of different people? What could I do myself in order to achieve cooperation through an open atmosphere – one in which everybody feels comfortable, where everyone can share their different opinions?

Making Shift Happen, a palette of behaviours and actions that you control yourself.

What choices do you make?

Afterword

During my upbringing, my father said to me, 'Be independent; never let someone else decide things for you.' Subsequently, when I was 10 years old, I was asked the question: 'What do you want to be when you grow up?' My answer to this was: 'The boss.' I didn't yet know what I wanted to be the boss of, but nevertheless my father taught me that this was my best option. All the advice I have been given in my life, and the advice provided by my educational mentors – whom I'm sure of spoke with good intentions – indicated to me that, as a girl, I would be better off choosing an alpha package (humanities) rather than a beta package (science and technology); I reacted to this advice in the same way: I must remain independent. Therefore the gamma package (social sciences and human behaviour) became my choice: human action and behaviour became my field of study, along with a specific focus on leadership and its impact.

Two men in my life have positively influenced me, and have encouraged me to build up my strengths and believe in myself: my father and my partner. Both instilled in me two essential values – no future without knowledge, and no business without contact.

Notes

1. See the definition by Ruijters and Simons in: Ruijters, M.C.P., Van de Braak, E.P.M., Draijer, H.M.A., Den Hartog, C., De Jonge, F., Van Luin, G.E.A., Van Oeffelt, T.P.A., Simons, P.R., Van de Veewey, M.H.C., & Wortelboer, F.Q.C. (2014), *Je binnenste buiten. Over professionele identiteit in organisaties.* Deventer: Vakmedianet. A professional is someone who chooses and is committed to continuously improving their service to customers in a competent and sincere manner, using his/her specialist knowledge and experience. In doing so, he/she makes use of, and actively contributes to, a community of fellow professionals who continuously develop the profession.
2. See Fowler & Christakis, 2008, for more information on emotional contagion.
3. McDermott, Fowler & Christakis, 2013.
4. Koene, 1996.
5. Argyris, 1990.
6. Barsade & O'Neill., 2016.
7. In: Fiske et al., 2002.
8. See Mayer et al., 2009.
9. In: Zenger et al., 2012.
10. These five personality dimensions were studied by, among others, Ernest Tupes and Raymond Christal, 1961.
11. Fiedler, 1967.
12. Bass, 1985.
13. Carlyle, 1840.
14. Stern 1970.
15. Francis, 2007.
16. Taylor, 1911.
17. Laloux, 2015.
18. Wilber K, *Een beknopte geschiedenis van alles* (1997). Rotterdam: Lemniscate.
19. Senge, 1990.
20. Scharmer, 2009.
21. Zenger & Folkman, 2009; Zenger & Folkman, 2019; Zenger et al., 2012.
22. Ericsson & Pool, 2017.
23. See Zenger & Folkman, 2013a.
24. De Wit, 2018.
25. Kwanten, 2019.
26. Collins 2001; Zenger & Folkman, 2009.
27. Drucker, 1954.
28. Laloux, 2015.
29. Covey, 1989.
30. Seligman 1990.

31.   Buckingham & Clifton, 2001.

32.   For more information, see Zenger & Folkman, 2012.

33.   See, among others, Wikipedia for further explanation.

34.   Van Muijen & Schaveling, 2011.

35.   For more information, see Goleman, 1995 and 2000.

36.   House & Howell, 1992; Conger, 1989.

37.   Bass, 1985.

38.   Den Hartog, Koopman & Van Muijen, 1997.

39.   Collins, 2001, p. 22.

40.   Collins, 2001.

41.   Hill et al., 2016.

42.   For more information, see Zenger & Folkman, 2013c; Zenger & Folkman, 2019.

43.   For more information, see Folkman, 2013.

44.   Laloux uses a paradigm of colours, where teals stands for organizations that actively organize themselves around an evolving goal that is constantly in development. This goal gives the organization the right to exist and is about the value it adds to the world. This is an iterative process in which all members of the organization actively listen to what the organization has to do in the world and act accordingly. See Laloux, 2015.

45.   For more information, see Folkman, 2013.

46.   Schmeier, 2020.

47.   Hirsch, 2019.

48.   De Waal, 2016.

49.   For more information, see Zenger & Folkman, 2015b.

50.   For more information, see Zenger & Folkman, 2016b.

51.   Koene, 1996.

52.   Goleman, Boyatzis & McKee, 2008.

53.   Goleman, Boyatzis & McKee, 2008.

54.   Bartel & Saavedra, 2000.

55.   For more information, see Zenger & Folkman, 2017.

56.   Arbo online, 2017.

57.   Nyberg, A., 2009.

58.   Sy, Côté & Saavedra, 2005.

59.   Cameron et al., 2011.

60.   Haidt, J.D., *The Righteous Mind: Why Good People are Divided by Politics and Religion* (2012). New York: Random House.

61.   Edmondson, Amy C., *The Fearless Organization* (2019). Amsterdam: Publisher Business Contact.

62.   Laloux, 2015.

63.   Zak, 2017.

64.   Zak, 2018.

65.   For more information, see Oreskovic, 2016.

66.   See studies by Laloux, 2015; Zak, 2018; De Waal, 2016; Cameron et al., 2011; Zenger & Folkman, 2019.

67. De Waal, A., 2016.
68. Ogbonna & Harris, 2000.
69. Kotter, 1988.
70. Hesket & Kotter, 1992.
71. Anthony, Viguerie & Waldeck, 2016.
72. Ogbonna & Harris, 2000.
73. Zenger et al., 2012.
74. Anseel & Devloo, 2009.
75. West & Farr, 1990.
76. Hülsheger, Anderson & Salgado, 2007; Patterson, 2009.
77. Stephens & Carmeli, 2007; Carmeli, Reiter-Palmon & Ziv, 2010; Javed et al., 2018.
78. For more information, see the Zenger & Folkman article https://hbr.org/2014/12/research-10-traits-of-innovative-leaders.
79. Hoffman, 1923.
80. Among others, by Yammarino & Atwater, 1993.
81. Vazire & Mehl, 2008.
82. For more information, see Zenger & Folkman, 2015a.
83. For more information, see Kay & Shipman, 2014.
84. Luft & Ingham, 1961.
85. Folkman, 2006.
86. Zenger & Folkman, 2014.
87. For more information, see Zenger & Folkman, 2013b.
88. Zenger & Stinnet, 2010.
89. Laloux, 2014.
90. De Wit, 2006.
91. Van Doorn, 2002.
92. Becker, 1997.
93. Verheijen, 2006.
94. Bontekoning, 2007.
95. De Wit, 2018.
96. CBE Group, 2009.
97. Prins, 2020.
98. Scholten, 2017.
99. Janka Stoker (1970). *Management Team*, 3 May 2019.
100. For more information, see Zenger & Folkman, 2016a.
101. Muusse, 2014.
102. Eagly & Karau, 2002.
103. Oakley, 2000.
104. Rudman & Glick, 2001.
105. Blaker et al., 2013.
106. Cuddy, Fiske & Glick, 2004.
107. Spencer, Steele & Quinn, 1999.
108. Aronson et al., 1999.
109. Stone et al., 1999.

110. Kay & Shipman, 2014.
111. Ibarra, Ely & Kolb, 2013.
112. Beentjes, 2016.
113. McKinsey, 2020.
114. Gallup, 2017.
115. Hurley & Shumway, 2015.
116. De Wit, 2018.
117. Kwanten, 2019.
118. Korn Ferry (2017). *Women CEOs Speak*. Retrieved 3 May 2019 from https: // engage.kornferry.com/Global/FileLib/Women_CEOs_speak/KFI_Rockefeller_Study_Women_CEOs_Speak.pdf
119. Draulans, 2002.
120. Woetzel et al., 2015.
121. Graven & Krishnan, 2018.
122. BlackLivesMatter: In 2013, Officer George Zimmerman was acquitted for the death of African-American youngster Trayvon Martin the previous year. Since then, the political activists of Black Lives Matter have been campaigning against all forms of violence against black people, including police brutality and ethnic profiling, and over-punishment of black people in the US legal system. The movement organizes demonstrations, protests, and has, since 2015, also challenged politicians to speak out against the violence against African Americans. (Source: Wikipedia)
123. Çelik, 2015; Çelik, 2018.
124. Ely & Thomas, 2001.
125. Çelik, 2016.
126. Ashikali & Groeneveld, 2015; OECD, 2015.
127. Çelik, 2020.
128. Gonzalez & DeNisi, 2009; Homan et al., 2008.
129. Shore et al., 2009.
130. Fujimoto, Härtel & Azmat, 2013.
131. Bilimori, Joy and Liang, 2008; Roberson, 2006.
132. For example, Mannix & Neale, 2005; Riordan, 2000.
133. Jackson, 1992a: Shore et al., 2009.
134. Avery et al., 2007; Gelfand et al., 2005; Ragins & Cornwell, 2001; Divorce, 2005; Wasserman, Gallegos & Ferdman, 2008.
135. Reskin, 2000.
136. Ashikali, 2015.
137. Nembhard & Edmondson, 2006.
138. Kreiner & Ashforth, 2004.
139. Acquavita et al., 2009.
140. Luzzo & McWhirter, 2001; Yap & Konrad, 2009.
141. Smith, 2005.
142. Lyness & Heilman, 2006.
143. Jeannet, 2000.
144. Stein & Book, 2011.

145. Ang et al., 2007; Van Dyne & Ang, 2005.
146. Anderson, 2014.
147. Shore et al., 2011.

Bibliography

Acquavita, S.P., Pittman, J., Gibbons, M., & Castellanos-Brown, K. (2009). Personal and organizational diversity factors 'impact on social workers' job satisfaction: Results from a national internet-based survey. *Administration in Social Work*, *33*(2), 151–166.

Aghina, W., Ahlback, K., De Smet, A., Lackey, G., Lurie, M., Murarka, M., & Handscomb, C. (2018). *The five trademarks of agile organizations*. Available at: www.mckinsey.com/business-functions/organization/our-insights/the-five-trademarks-of-agile-organizations. [Accessed 18/10/2020].

Agrawal, V. (2012). Managing the diversified team: challenges and strategies for improving performance. *Team Performance Management*, *18*(7/8), 384–400.

Anderson, D.L. (2014). *Organization development: The process of leading organizational change* (3rd ed.). Thousand Oaks, CA: Sage.

Ang, S., Van Dyne, L., Koh, C., Ng, K.Y., Templer, K.J., Tay, C., & Chandrasekar, N.A. (2007). Cultural intelligence: Its measurement and effects on cultural judgment and decision making, cultural adaptation, and task performance. *Management and Organization Review*, *3*(3), 335–371.

Anseel, F. & Devloo, T. (2009). Stimuleren van innovatief werkgedrag in organisaties: Een overzicht van empirische bevindingen. In R. Van Rossem, K. Vandevelde, & H. De Grande (Eds.), *Kennis in wording* (pp. 143–162). Gent: Human Resources in Research (UGent).

Anthony, S.D., Viguerie, P., & Waldeck, A. (2016). *Corporate Longevity: Turbulence ahead for large organizations*. Innosight. https://www.innosight.com/wp-content/uploads/2016/08/Corporate-Longevity-2016-Final.pdf. [Accessed 18/10/2020].

Arbo online (2017). *Dit zijn de meest voorkomende beroepsziekten*. www.arbo-online.nl/gezond-werken/nieuws/2017/09/dit-zijn-de-meest-voorkomende-beroepsziekten-101520. [Accessed 18/10/2020].

Argyris, C. (1990). *Overcoming organizational defenses: Facilitating organizational learning* (1st ed.). London: Pearson Education.

Aronson, J., Lustina, M.J., Good, C., Keough, K., Steele, C.M., & Brown, J. (1999). When white men can't do math: Necessary and sufficient factors in stereotype threat. *Journal of experimental social psychology*, *35*(1), 29–46.

Ashikali, T. & Groeneveld, S. (2015). Diversity management in public organizations and its effect on employees' affective commitment: The role of transformational leadership and the inclusiveness of the organizational culture. *Review of Public Personnel Administration*, *35*(2), 146–168.

Avery, D.R., McKay, P.F., Wilson, D.C., & Tonidandel, S. (2007). Unequal attendance: The relationships between race, organizational diversity cues, and absenteeism. *Personnel Psychology*, *60*(4), 875–902.

Barsade, S. & O'Neill, O.A. (2016). Manage your emotional culture. *Harvard Business Review*, January–February, 58–66.

Bartel, C.A. & Saavedra, R. (2000). The collective construction of work group moods. *Administrative Science Quarterly*, 45(2), 197–231.

Bass, B.M. (1985). *Leadership and Performance Beyond Expectations*. New York: Collier Macmillan.

Bass, B.M. (1998). *Transformational leadership: Industrial, military, and educational impact*. New York: Lawrence Erlbaum Associates.

Becker, H. (1997). *De toekomst van de Verloren Generatie*. Amsterdam: MeulenhoffBoekerij.

Beentjes, J. (2016). *2 op 3 kandidaten haken af bij ingewikkelde sollicitatieprocedure*. *PW.*, www.pwnet.nl/instroom/nieuws/2016/10/2-op-3-kandidaten-haken-af-bij-ingewikkelde-sollicitatieprocedure-10122622. [Accessed 18/10/2020].

Bilimoria, D., Joy, S., & Liang, X. (2008). Breaking barriers and creating inclusiveness: Lessons of organizational transformation to advance women faculty in academic science and engineering. *Human Resource Management*, 47(3), 423–441.

Blaker, N.M., Rompa, I., Dessing, I.H., Vriend, A.F., Herschberg, C., & Van Vugt, M. (2013). The height leadership advantage in men and women: Testing evolutionary psychology predictions about the perceptions of tall leaders. *Group Processes & Intergroup Relations*, 16(1), 17–27.

Bontekoning, A.C. (2007). *Generaties in organisaties* [Doctoral thesis]. Universiteit van Tilburg.

Bourne, K. (2009). The inclusion breakthrough: Unleashing the real power of diversity. In C. Harvey & J. Allard (Eds.), *Understanding and managing diversity* (4th ed., pp. 263–270). Upper Saddle River, NJ: Prentice Hall.

Buckingham, M. & Clifton, D.O. (2001). *Now, discover your strengths*. New York: Simon & Schuster.

Cameron, K., Mora, C., Leutscher, T., & Calarco, M. (2011). Effects of positive practices on organizational effectiveness. *The Journal of Applied Behavioral Science*, 47(3), 266–308.

Carlyle, T. (1840). *On heroes, hero-worship and the heroic in history*. London: James Fraser.

Carmeli, A., Reiter-Palmon, R., & Ziv, E. (2010). Inclusive leadership and employee involvement in creative tasks in the workplace: The mediating role of psychological safety. *Creativity Research Journal*, 22(3), 250–260.

CBE Group (2009). Mijn loopbaan, wat verwacht de nieuwe professional van zijn baan?

Çelik, S. (2015). De business case van diversiteit in de publieke context: de verbindende overheid. *Tijdschrift voor HRM*, 3(2), 1–33.

Çelik, S. (2016). *Sturen op verbinden: De business case van diversiteit van publieke organisaties*. Rotterdam: Optima Grafische Communicatie. https://kennis-openbaarbestuur.nl/media/255616/sturen-op-verbinden-de-business-case-van-diversiteit-van-publieke-organisaties.pdf. [Accessed 18/10/2020].

Çelik, S. (2018). *Diversiteit, de gewoonste zaak van de wereld?* Lecture, Hogeschool Leiden, Leiden.

Çelik, (2020). *Inclusie is een individuele keuze, ook in tijden van crisis.* https://www.scienceguide.nl/2020/04/inclusie-is-een-individuele-keuze-ook-in-tijden-van-crisis/. [Accessed 18/10/2020].

Collins, J.C. (2001). *Good to great: Why some companies make the leap and others don't.* New York: Harper Collins.

Conger, J.A. (1989). *The charismatic leader: Behind the mystique of exceptional leadership.* San Francisco: Jossey-Bass.

Cotter, D.A., Hermsen, J.M., Ovadia, S., & Vanneman, R. (2001). The glass ceiling effect. *Social Forces, 80*(2), 655–681.

Covey, S. (1989). *The 7 habits of highly effective people: Powerful lessons in personal change.* New York: Simon & Schuster.

Craft Research (n.d.) *Fortune 500 – Gender diversity of top management.* https://craft.co/reports/fortune-500-gender-diversity. [Accessed 18/10/2020].

Cuddy, A.J., Fiske, S.T., & Glick, P. (2004). When professionals become mothers, warmth doesn't cut the ice. *Journal of Social issues, 60*(4), 701–718.

De Waal, A. (2016). *Hoe bouw je een High Performance Organisatie? De vijf universele factoren van excellent presteren.* Culemborg: Van Duuren Management.

De Wit, M.J.E. (2006). *Generatiemanagement Utrecht*: CBE Group BV.

De Wit, M.J.E. (2018). *De staat van de Nederlandse onderwijsleider.* Utrecht: Academica, via https://wij-leren.nl/de-staat-van-de-nederlandse-onderwijsleider.php. [Accessed 18/10/2020].

Den Hartog, D.N., Koopman, P.L., & Van Muijen, J.J. (1997). *Inspirerend leiderschap in organisaties.* Schoonhoven: Academic Service.

Douglas, C., Ferris, G.R., Buckley, M.R., & Gundlach, M.J. (2003). Organizational and social influences on leader-member exchange processes: Implications for the management of diversity. In G. Graen (Ed.), *Dealing with diversity* (pp. 59–90). Greenwich, CT: Information Age Publishing.

Draulans, V.J.R. (2002). Glazen plafond: realiteit of mythe? Een genderanalyse van leidinggeven. *Uitgelezen: driemaandelijkse uitgave van Rol en Samenleving VZW (RoSa), 8*(4), 2–13.

Drucker, P.F. (1954). *The practice of management.* New York: Harper Collins.

Eagly, A.H. & Karau, S.J. (2002). Role congruity theory of prejudice toward female leaders. *Psychological review, 109*(3), 573.

Earley, P.C. & Peterson, R.S. (2004). The elusive cultural chameleon: Cultural intelligence as a new approach to intercultural training for the global manager. *Academy of Management Learning & Education, 3*(1), 100–115.

Eisenberger, N.I., Lieberman, M.D., & Williams, K.D. (2003). Does rejection hurt? An FMRI study of social exclusion. *Science, 302*(5643), 290–292.

Ely, R.J. & Thomas, D.A. (2001). Cultural diversity at work: The effects of diversity perspectives on work group processes and outcomes. *Administrative Science Quarterly, 46*(2), 229–273.

Ericsson, A. & Pool, R. (2017). *Piek. Hoe gewone mensen buitengewoon kunnen presteren.* Amsterdam: Unieboek/Spectrum.

Fiedler, F.E. (1967). *A theory of leadership effectiveness.* New York: McGraw-Hill.

Fiske, S.T., Cuddy, A.J., Glick, P., & Xu, J. (2002). A model of (often mixed) stereotype content: Competence and warmth respectively follow from perceived status and competition. *Journal of Personality and Social Psychology, 82*(6), 878.

Folkman, J.R. (2006). *The power of feedback: 35 principles for turning feedback from others into personal and professional change.* Hoboken: Wiley.

Folkman, J.R. (2013). *Everything counts: The 6 ways to inspire and motivate top performance.* Forbes.com, www.forbes.com/sites/joefolkman/2013/05/20/everything-counts-the-6-ways-to-inspire-and-motivate-top-performance/#2292c42d25e1. [Accessed 18/10/2020].

Fowler, J.H. & Christakis, N.A. (2008). Dynamic spread of happiness in a large social network: Longitudinal analysis over 20 years in the Framingham heart study. *British Medical Journal, 337*(a2338), 1–9. Available at: www.bmj.com/content/bmj/337/bmj.a2338.full.pdf. [Accessed 18/10/2020].

Francis, M. (2007). *Herbert Spencer and the invention of modern life.* New York: Cornell University Press.

Fujimoto, Y., Härtel, C.E., & Azmat, F. (2013). Towards a diversity justice management model: Integrating organizational justice and diversity management. *Social Responsibility Journal. 9*(1), 148–166.

Gallup press (2017). *State of the global workplace.* https://www.gallup.com/workplace/238079/state-global-workplace-2017.aspx. [Accessed 18/10/2020].

Gelfand, M.J., Nishii, L., Raver, L., & Schneider, B. (2005). Discrimination in the workplace: An organizational-level analysis. In R. Dipboye & A. Collella (Eds.), *Psychological and Organizational Bases of Discrimination at Work* (pp. 89–116). Mahwah, NJ: Lawrence Erlbaum Associates.

Gerndt, U. (2014). *Frederic Laloux 'Reinventing organizations' – Excerpt and summaries.* Munich: Change factory. http://www.reinventingorganizations.com/uploads/2/1/9/8/21988088/140305_laloux_reinventing_organizations.pdf. [Accessed 18/10/2020].

Goleman, D. (1995). *Emotional intelligence: Why it can matter more than IQ.* New York: Bantam Books.

Goleman, D. (2000). Leadership that gets results. *Harvard Business Review, 78*(2), 4–17.

Goleman, D., Boyatzis, R., & McKee, A. (2008). *Primal leadership: Realizing the power of emotional intelligence.* Brighton: Harvard Business Review Press.

Gonzalez, J.A. & DeNisi. AS. (2009). Cross-level effects of demography and diversity climate on organizational attachment and firm effectiveness. *Journal of Organizational Behavior, 30*(1), 21–40.

Graven, W. & Krishnan, M. (2018). *The power of parity: Het potentieel pakken: de waarde van meer gelijkheid tussen mannen en vrouwen op de Nederlandse arbeidsmarkt.* New York: McKeinsey Global Institute.

Hesket, J.L. & Kotter, J.P. (1992). *Corporate Culture and Performance.* New York: Free Press.

Hill, A., Mellon, L., Laker, B., & Goddard, J. (2016). The one type of leader who can turn around a failing school. *Harvard Business Review.* https://hbr.org/2016/10/the-one-type-of-leader-who-can-turn-around-a-failing-school. [Accessed 18/10/2020].

Hirsch, E. D. (2019). *Why knowledge matters: Rescuing our children from failed educational theories.* Harvard Education Press.

Hoffman, G.J. (1923). An experiment in self-estimation. *The Journal of Abnormal Psychology and Social Psychology, 18*(1), 43–49. In C.F.M.C. Aarts (1964). *Zelfbeoordelingen* [proefschrift Radboud University]

Homan, A.C., Hollenbeck, J.R., Humphrey, S.E., van Knippenberg, D., Ilgen, D.R., & Van Kleef, G.A. (2008). Facing differences with an open mind: Openness to experience, salience of intragroup differences, and performance of various work groups. *Academy of Management Journal, 51*(6), 1204–1222.

House, R.J. & Howell, J.M. (1992). Personality and charismatic leadership. *The Leadership Quarterly, 3*(2), 81–108.

Hülsheger, U., Anderson, N., & Salgado, J. (2009). Team-level predictors of innovation at work: A comprehensive meta-analysis spanning three decades of research. *The Journal of Applied Psychology, 94*(5), 1128–1145.

Hurley, K. & Shumway, P. (2015). *Real women, real leaders: Surviving and succeeding in the business world.* Hoboken: Wiley.

Ibarra, H., Ely, R.J., & Kolb, D.M. (2013). Women rising: The unseen barriers. *Harvard Business Review.* https://hbr.org/2013/09/women-rising-the-unseen-barriers. [Accessed 18/10/2020].

Jackson, S.E., Brett, J.F., Sessa, V.I., Cooper, D.M., Julia, J.A., & Peyronnin, K. (1991). Some differences make a difference: Individual dissimilarity and group heterogeneity as correlates of recruitment, promotions, and turnover. *Journal of Applied Psychology, 76*(5), 675–689.

Jackson, S.E. (1992) Consequences of group composition for the interpersonal dynamics of strategic issue processing. In J. Dutton, A. Huff, & P., Shrivastava (Eds.), *Advances in strategic management* (pp. 345–382), Greenwich: JAI Press.

Jeannet, J. (2000). *Managing with a global mindset.* London: Pearson Education.

Jokinen, T. (2005). Global leadership competencies: A review and discussion. *Journal of European Industrial Training, 29*(2–3), 199–216.

Kay, K. & Shipman, C. (2014). The confidence gap. *The Atlantic.* https://www.theatlantic.com/magazine/archive/2014/05/the-confidence-gap/359815/. [Accessed 18/10/2020].

Koene, B.A.S. (1996). *Organizational culture, leadership, and performance in context: Trust and rationality in organizations.* [Doctoral thesis.] University of Limburg.

Kotter, J.P. (1988). *Leading Change: An action plan from the world's foremost expert on business leadership.* Cambridge, MA: Harvard Business School Publishing.

Kouzes, J.M. & Posner, B.Z. (2012). *The leadership challenge* (5th ed.). San Francisco: Jossey-Bass.

Kreiner, G.E. & Ashforth, B.E. (2004). Evidence toward an expanded model of organizational identification. *Journal of Organizational Behavior, 25*(1), 1–27.

Kwanten, K. (2019). *The impact of principal leadership on teacher engagement and student achievement scores in primary schools in the Netherlands.* [Thesis.] Vrije Universiteit Amsterdam.

Laloux, F. (2014). *Reinventing organizations: Human development. overview of the main (organizational) paradigms.* http://www.reinventingorganizations.

com/uploads/2/1/9/8/21988088/140305_laloux_reinventing_organizations. pdf. [Accessed 18/10/2020].

Laloux, F. (2014). *Reinventing organizations: A guide to creating organizations inspired by the next stage in human consciousness.* Millis: Nelson Parker.

Luft, J. & Ingham, H. (1961). The Johari Window: A graphic model of awareness in interpersonal relations. *Human Relations Training News,* 5(9), 6–7.

Luzzo, D.A. & McWhirter, E.H. (2001). Sex and ethnic differences in the perception of educational and career-related barriers and levels of coping efficacy. *Journal of Counseling and Development,* 79(1), 61–68.

Lyness, K.S. & Heilman, M.E. (2006). When fit is fundamental: Performance evaluations and promotions of upper-level female and male managers. *Journal of Applied Psychology,* 91(4), 777–785.

Management Team, (3 May 2019). *Hebben millennials echt een aparte millennial aanpak nodig?* https://www.mt.nl/management-team/millenials-aparte-millennial-aanpak-management/570495. [Accessed 18/10/2020].

Mannix, E. & Neale, M.A. (2005). What differences make a difference? The promise and reality of diverse teams in organizations. *Psychological Science in the Public Interest,* 6(2), 31–55.

Mavrinac, M.A. (2005). Transformational leadership: Peer mentoring as a values-based learning process. *Portal: Libraries and the Academy,* 5(3), 391–404.

Mayer, D.M., Kuenzi, M., Greenbaum, R., Bardes, M., & Salvador, R.B. (2009). How low does ethical leadership flow? Test of a trickle-down model. *Organizational Behavior and Human Decision Processes,* 108(1), 1–13.

McDermott, R., Fowler, J.H., & Christakis, N.A. (2013). Breaking up is hard to do, unless everyone else is doing it too: Social network effects on divorce in a longitudinal sample. *Social Forces; A Scientific Medium of Social Study and Interpretation,* 92(2), 491–519. https://doi.org/10.1093/sf/sot096.

McKinsey, (2020) *Bedrijven met diversiteit in de top maken meer winst.* https://www. consultancy.nl/nieuws/29705/mckinsey-bedrijven-met-diversiteit-in-de-top-maken-meer-winst. [Accessed 18/10/2020].

Muusse, T. (2014). *Duurzaam leiderschap van Generatie Y.* Erasmus Universiteit.

Nyberg, A. (2009). The impact of managerial leadership on stress and health among employees. https://openarchive.ki.se/xmlui/bitstream/handle/10616/38102/ thesis.pdf?sequence=1&isAllowed=y. [Accessed 18/10/2020].

Oakley, J.G. (2000). Gender-based barriers to senior management positions: Understanding the scarcity of female CEOs. *Journal of Business Ethics,* 27(4), 321–334.

OECD. (2015). Managing a diverse public administration and effectively responding to the needs of a more diverse workforce. France: Organization for Economic Co-operation and Development.

Ogbonna, E. & Harris, L.C. (2000). Leadership style, organizational culture and performance: empirical evidence from UK companies. *The International Journal of Human Resource Management,* 11(4), 766–788.

Oreskovic, A. (2016). Twitter is having an internal pep-rally meeting to pump up employees. Business Insider. www.businessinsider.com/twitter-employees-tweeting-in-support-of-the-company-2016-1. [Accessed 18/10/2020].

Patterson, F. Kerrin, M., & Gatto-Roissard, G. (2009). *Characteristics & behaviors of innovative people in organizations*. London: City, University of London.

Prins, D. (2020). *Oorzaak van burn-out en depressie bij millennials: wat is er echt aan de hand?* AD. https://www.ad.nl/gezond/oorzaak-van-burn-out-en-depressie-bij-millennials-wat-is-er-echt-aan-de-hand~adbc8513. [Accessed 18/10/2020].

Ragins, B.R. & Cornwell, J.M. (2001). Pink triangles: Antecedents and consequences of perceived workplace discrimination against gay and lesbian employees. *Journal of Applied Psychology, 86*(6): 1244–1261.

Reskin, B.F. (2000). Getting it right: Sex and race inequality in work organizations. *Annual Review of Sociology, 26*(1), 707–709.

Riordan, C.M. (2000). Relational demography within groups: Past developments, contradictions, and new directions. *Research in Personnel and Human Resources Management, 19*, 131–173.

Riordan, C.M. & Wayne, J.H. (2008). A review and examination of demographic similarity measures used to assess relational demography within groups. *Organizational Research Methods, 11*(3), 562–592.

Roberson, Q.M (2006). Disentangling the meanings of diversity and inclusion in organizations. *Group and Organization Management, 31*(2), 212–236.

Rudman, L.A. & Glick, P. (2001). Prescriptive gender stereotypes and backlash toward agentic women. *Journal of Social Issues, 57*(4), 743–762.

Ryan, J. (2000). Inclusive leadership and social justice. *Leadership and Policy in Schools, 5*(3), 317.

Scharmer, C.O. (2009). *Theory U – Leading from the future as it emerges*. San Francisco: Berrett-Koehler.

Scheid, T.L. (2005). Stigma as a barrier to employment: Mental disability and the Americans with disabilities act. *International Journal of Law and Psychiatry, 28*(6), 670–690.

Schmeier, M. (2020). *Bordwerk en aantekeningen: Slow teaching in de 21e eeuw*. Amsterdam: Pica.

Scholten, J. (2017). *Het Millennial mysterie. Jong, kansrijk, gedreven en toch niet tevreden*. Amsterdam: Water.

Seligman, M.E.P. (1990). *Learned optimism: How to change your mind and your life*. New York: Alfred A. Knopf.

Senge, P. (1990). *The Fifth discipline: The art and practice of the learning organization*. New York: Doubleday/Currency.

Shore, L.M., Chung-Herrera, B.G., Dean, M.A., Ehrhart, K.H., Jung, D.I., Randel, A.E., & Singh, G. (2009). Diversity in organizations: Where are we now and where are we going? *Human resource management review, 19*(2), 117–133.

Shore, L.M., Randel, A.M., Chung, B.M., Dean, M.A., Ehrhart, K.H., & Singh, G. (2011). Inclusion and diversity in work groups: A review and model for future research. *Journal of Management, 34*(4), 1262–1289.

Smith, R.A. (2005). Do the determinants of promotion differ for White men versus women and minorities? *The American Behavioral Scientist, 48*(9), 1157–1181.

Spencer, S.J., Steele, C.M., & Quinn, D.M. (1999). Stereotype threat and women's math performance. *Journal of Experimental Social Psychology, 35*(1), 4–28.

Stein, S.J. & Book, H.E. (2011). *The EQ edge: Emotional intelligence and your success* (3rd ed.), Mississauga: Jossey-Bass.

Stephens, J. & Carmeli, A. (2015). *Relational leadership and creativity: The effects of respectful engagement and caring on meaningfulness and creative work involvement.* doi:10.4337/9781784715465.00021.

Stern, F. (1970). *The varieties of history: from Voltaire to the present.* New York: Macmillan Publishers.

Stone, J., Lynch, CI, Sjomeling, M., & Darley, J.M. (1999). Stereotype threat effects on black and white athletic performance. *Journal of Personality and Social Psychology, 77*(6), 1213–1227.

Sy, T., Côté, S., & Saavedra, R. (2005). The contagious leader: impact of the leader's mood on the mood of group members, group affective tone, and group processes. *Journal of Applied Psychology, 90*(2), 295–305.

Taylor, F.W. (1911). *The principles of scientific management.* New York/London: Harper & Brothers.

Tupes, E.C. & Christal, R.E. (1961). *Recurrent personality factors based on trait ratings.* Technical report. DTIC Document. https://apps.dtic.mil/dtic/tr/fulltext/u2/267778. pdf. [Accessed 18/10/2020].

Van Doorn, J.A.A. (2002). *Gevangen in de tijd. Over generaties en hun geschiedenis.* Amsterdam: Boom.

Van Dyne, L. & Ang, S. (2005). Getting more than you expect: Global leader initiative to span structural holes and reputation effectiveness. *Advances in Global Leadership, 4*, 101–122.

Van Muijen, J.J. & Schaveling, J. (2011). Leiderschap: Een theoretisch overzicht. *M & O: Tijdschrift voor management en organisatie, 65*(4), 6–26.

Vazire, S. & Mehl, M.R. (2008). Knowing me, knowing you: The accuracy and unique predictive validity of self-ratings and other-ratings of daily behavior. *Journal of Personality and Social Psychology, 95*(5), 1202–1216.

Verheijen, T. (2006). Het *démasqué* van de generatiekloof. *Nederlands tijdschrift voor coaching, 3*, 23–26.

Wasserman, I.C., Gallegos, P.V., & Ferdman, B.M. (2008). Dancing with resistance: Leadership challenges in fostering a culture of inclusion. In K.M. Thomas (Ed.), *Diversity resistance in organizations* (pp. 175–200). New York: Taylor & Francis.

West, M.A. & Farr, J.L. (1990). *Innovation and creativity at work: Psychological and organizational strategies.* Hoboken: John Wiley & Sons.

Woetzel, J., Madgavkar, A., Ellingrud, K., Labaye, E., Devillard, PS, Kutcher, E., & Krishnan, M. (2015). *The power of parity: How advancing women's equality can add $12 trillion to global growth.* New York: McKinsey Global Institute.

Yammarino, F.J. & Atwater, L.E. (1993). Understanding self-perception accuracy: Implications for human resource management. *Human Resource Management, 32*(2–3), 231–247.

Yap, M. & Konrad, A.M. (2009). Gender and racial differentials in promotions: Is there a sticky floor, a mid-level bottleneck, or a glass ceiling? *Industrial Relations, 64*(4), 593–619.

Zak, P.J. (2017). The neuroscience of trust. *Harvard Business Review, 95*(1), 84–90.

Zak, P.J. (2018). The neuroscience of high-trust organizations. *Consulting Psychology Journal: Practice and Research, 70*(1), 45–58.

Zenger, J.H. & Folkman, J.R. (2009). *The extraordinary leader: Turning good managers into great leaders.* New York: McGraw-Hill.

Zenger, J.H. & Folkman, J.R. (2013a). Bad leaders can change their spots. *Harvard Business Review,* https://hbr.org/2013/01/good-news-poor-leaders-can-cha. [Accessed 18/10/2020].

Zenger, J.H. & Folkman, J.R. (2013b). Overcoming feedback phobia: Take the first step. *Harvard Business Review,* https://hbr.org/2013/12/overcoming-feedback-phobia-take-the-first-step. [Accessed 18/10/2020].

Zenger, J.H. & Folkman, J.R. (2013c). What Inspiring Leaders Do. Forbes.com, https://hbr.org/2013/06/what-inspiring-leaders-do. [Accessed 18/10/2020].

Zenger, J.H. & Folkman, J.R. (2014). *The power of feedback: 35 principles for turning feedback from others into personal and professional change.* Hoboken: Wiley.

Zenger, J.H. & Folkman, J.R. (2015a). We like leaders who underrate themselves. *Harvard Business Review,* https://hbr.org/2015/11/we-like-leaders-who-underrate-themselves. [Accessed 18/10/2020].

Zenger, J.H. & Folkman, J.R. (2015b). You have to be fast to be seen as a great leader. *Harvard Business Review,* https://hbr.org/2015/02/you-have-to-be-fast-to-be-seen-as-a-great-leader. [Accessed 18/10/2020].

Zenger, J.H. & Folkman, J.R (2016a). How age and gender affect self-improvement. *Harvard Business Review,* https://hbr.org/2016/01/how-age-and-gender-affect-self-improvement. [Accessed 18/10/2020].

Zenger, J.H. & Folkman, J.R. (2016b). The traits of leaders who do things fast and well. *Harvard Business Review,* https://hbr.org/2016/11/the-traits-of-leaders-who-do-thingsfast-and-well. [Accessed 18/10/2020].

Zenger, J.H. & Folkman, J.R. (2017). How managers drive results and employee engagement at the same time. *Harvard Business Review,* https://hbr.org/2017/06/how-managers-drive-results-and-employee-engagement-at-the-same-time. [Accessed 18/10/2020].

Zenger, J.H. & Folkman, J.R., (5 February 2019). The 3 elements of trust. *Harvard Business Review.* https://hbr.org/2019/02/the-3-elements-of-trust. [Accessed 18/10/2020].

Zenger, J.H. & Folkman, J.R. (2019). *The new extraordinary leader: Turning good managers into great leaders.* New York: McGraw-Hill.

Zenger, J.H. & Stinnet, K. (2010). *The extraordinary coach: How the best leaders help others grow.* New York: McGraw-Hill.

Zenger, J.H., Folkman, J.R., Sherwin, R.H., & Steel, B.A. (2012). *How to be exceptional: Drive leadership success by magnifying your strengths.* New York: McGraw-Hill.